Woodworking
Tools & Techniques

An Introduction to Basic Woodworking

by Chris Marshall

CREATIVE
PUBLISHING
international

CHANHASSEN, MINNESOTA

www.creativepub.com

CONTENTS

© Copyright 2004
Creative Publishing international, Inc.
18705 Lake Drive East
Chanhassen, Minnesota 55317
1-800-328-3895
www.creativepub.com

Printed by Quebecor World
10 9 8 7 6 5 4 3 2 1

President/CEO: Michael Eleftheriou
Vice President/Publisher: Linda Ball
Vice President/Retail Sales & Marketing: Kevin Haas

Executive Editor: Bryan Trandem
Creative Director: Tim Himsel
Managing Editor: Michelle Skudlarek
Editorial Director: Jerri Farris

Author: Chris Marshall
Editor: Brett Martin
Senior Art Director: David Schelitzche
Copy Editor: Shannon Zemlicka
Project Manager: Tracy Stanley
Technical Photo Editor: Randy Austin
Mac Production: Jon Simpson
Illustrators: David Schelitzche, Jon Simpson, Earl Slack
Photo Researcher: Julie Caruso
Studio Services Manager: Jeanette Moss McCurdy
Photographer: Tate Carlson
Scene Shop Carpenter: Randy Austin
Director of Production Services and Photography: Kim Gerber
Production Manager: Helga Thielen

WOODWORKING TOOLS & TECHNIQUES

Other titles from Creative Publishing international include:

The New Everyday Home Repairs; Basic Wiring & Electrical Repairs; Building Decks; Home Masonry Projects & Repairs; Workshop Tips & Techniques; Bathroom Remodeling; Flooring Projects & Techniques; Decorative Accessories; Kitchen Accessories; Maximizing Minimal Space; Outdoor Wood Furnishings; Easy Wood Furniture Projects; Customizing Your Home; Carpentry: Remodeling; Carpentry: Tools • Shelves • Walls • Doors; Exterior Home Repairs & Improvements; Home Plumbing Projects & Repairs; Advanced Home Wiring; Advanced Deck Building; Built-In Projects for the Home; Landscape Design & Construction; Refinishing & Finishing Wood; Building Porches & Patios; Advanced Home Plumbing; Remodeling Kitchens; Finishing Basements & Attics; Stonework & Masonry Projects; Sheds, Gazebos & Outbuildings; Building & Finishing Walls & Ceilings; Customizing Your Home; The Complete Guide to Home Plumbing; The Complete Guide to Home Wiring; The Complete Guide to Building Decks; The Complete Guide to Painting & Decorating; The Complete Guide to Creative Landscapes; The Complete Guide to Home Masonry; The Complete Guide to Home Carpentry; The Complete Guide to Home Storage; The Complete Guide to Windows & Doors; The Complete Guide to Bathrooms; The Complete Guide to Easy Woodworking Projects; The Complete Guide to Flooring; The Complete Guide to Ceramic & Stone Tile; The Complete Photo Guide to Home Repair; The Complete Photo Guide to Home Improvement; The Complete Photo Guide to Outdoor Home Improvement; Accessible Home; Open House; Lighting Design & Installation

Library of Congress
Cataloging-in-Publication Data

ISBN 1-58923-096-5

PHOTOGRAPHY CONTRIBUTORS

Binkeys Woodworking
Dave Vincent
www.binkeyswoodworking.com

DeWALT
800-433-9258
www.dewalt.com

Georgia-Pacific Corp.
1-800-BUILD GP
www.gp.com

Woodcraft Supply Corp.
800-535-4482
www.woodcraft.com

Other Photography Credits
Corbis Professional Licensing
http://pro.corbis.com
©Phillip Gould/Corbis: p. 24

Introduction

Ever walk through a furniture gallery or craft fair and wish you could build wood furniture or other projects yourself? What's holding you back?

If the answer has to do with the absence of a workshop or lack of the "right" equipment, you'd be surprised how much woodworking can be done in small spaces with a modest collection of tools. Maybe you don't feel like a particularly talented or creative sort. Don't fret. There are thousands of published plans available for building beautiful furniture and accessories by the numbers. With a little patience and a good set of plans, you don't have to be da Vinci to build something you'll treasure. It could be that woodworking is one of those hobbies you want to pursue once the kids are grown and moved away or when retirement comes. But wouldn't it be fun to start that hobby now, even in a limited way, to whet your appetite for those long, leisurely days in the shop when time is on your side? Even the busiest schedule still allows a bit of time for woodworking.

Whether you have yet to buy your first tool, or are dabbling in woodworking already but want to learn more, this book is for you. Chapter by chapter, *Woodworking Tools & Techniques* is organized to help you get started in what we hope will be a lifelong hobby. From setting up a home workshop and buying the proper tools through choosing wood and designing your first projects, you'll find helpful advice here. You'll learn how to make parts using a variety of different tools, assemble them sensibly to ensure success, and even select and apply the best finishes. Hundreds of full-color photos and illustrations plus clear, easy-to-follow text will guide you each step of the way. Keep this book handy, even as your skills grow. You'll surely return to it again and again.

NOTICE TO READERS

This book provides useful instructions, but we cannot anticipate all of your working conditions or the characteristics of your materials and tools. For safety, you should use caution, care, and good judgment when following the procedures described in this book. Consider your own skill level and the instructions and safety precautions associated with the various tools and materials shown. The publisher cannot assume responsibility for any damage to property, injury to persons, or losses incurred as a result of misuse of the information provided.

Chapter 1
DEVELOPING A HOME WORKSHOP

Woodworking is one of those hobbies that demands space. Whether you're planning to just tinker on an occasional project or pursue woodworking more ambitiously, you're going to need a certain amount of room to store tools, lumber, and projects at various stages of completion. Even casual woodworking has a way of building on itself. Small boxes of tools seem to bloom into more and larger tools that eat up floor space. Other workshop items, such as a workbench, lumber rack, and cabinets for tools, will also enter the picture. No matter how much space you dedicate to a shop, it fills up in the end.

Woodworking is a messy and often noisy pastime. Sawing, sanding, planing, and drilling create plenty of debris and airborne dust. Wood glues and finishes inevitably drip and spill, and some produce irritating and even hazardous fumes. A workshop offers you space to be creative even if you make a mess. It also provides a place with some degree of isolation from the rest of the household for operating power tools. The quieter you can work, the happier everyone around you will be about your new hobby.

So what's a reasonable workspace for woodworking? Let's assume for the moment that you are a budding woodworker setting up your first home workshop. This chapter will help you identify the likely spaces in your home that could become workshops and weigh the pros and cons of each option. We'll review what your needs for lighting, electricity, climate, and dust control will be, then suggest a core group of tools and other furnishings to help you tackle a wide variety of projects. Finally, we'll lay some ground rules for shop safety before moving ahead into the technique-building chapters that follow. If you've already established your shop, skim this chapter for helpful hints. Be sure to read the safety section on pages 21 to 23. It never hurts to review safety procedures even if you discover that you already follow them.

Choosing a shop space

Whether you rent or own your home, and regardless of the region in which you live, there's bound to be space for a workshop if you think creatively. Even a small area can become an effective shop if you plan the space carefully and stay organized. The usual shop locations include basements, garage stalls, barns, and machine sheds or other outbuildings. Three-season porches and garden sheds also make decent shops under the right circumstances. Depending on the type of woodworking you do, you may be able to work outside on occasion to expand your workspace. Your choices for a shop will be influenced by factors such as climate and noise control, material handling, tool portability, access to electricity, and other sorts of storage limitations. We'll discuss each of these issues as they impact the following common workshop locations.

Basement shops: If you live in a northern region with cold winters, a basement shop offers the luxury of climate control. Nothing will chill you to the bone as quickly as handling metal tools in the dead of January in an unheated workshop. Your furnace will keep workshop conditions pleasant all winter, and a below-grade basement shop will stay comfortably cool during summer's worst heat. If your home was built within the past 30 to 40 years, it probably has a ceiling that's high enough to keep you from bumping your head on suspended ductwork or plumbing. Ceilings should be at least 7 feet high in a shop, and the higher the better for maneuvering long boards or sheets of plywood. Basement shops are typically close to your home's main electrical service panel, so electrical outlets are easy to add if the shop needs more.

Despite the pleasant climate and convenient location, basement shops can have drawbacks. If your basement stairwell is narrow or steep, it can be difficult and even dangerous to carry heavy building materials and large tools up and down the stairs. Finding enough room to cut long lumber or wide sheet materials can also be challenging in a basement shop. Older basements may have numerous posts supporting the floor joists that limit the amount of open space you have available.

If the laundry room is in the basement, you probably won't want

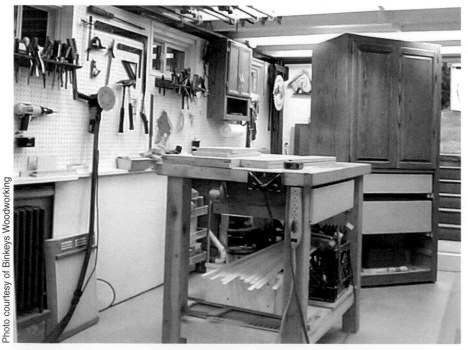

Photo courtesy of Binkeys Woodworking

With ample overhead lighting and sufficiently high ceilings, basements can offer pleasant, warm spaces for woodworking.

sawdust mixing with freshly laundered clothes. Fine dust and fumes from wood finishes shouldn't mingle with the pilot lights on furnaces, water heaters, and gas clothes dryers, either. In high concentrations, dust or fumes can combust. Some types of adhesives and finishes produce fumes that are heavier than air, so they'll be trapped in a basement shop unless you have fans and windows to circulate the air. This says nothing for the smells that will waft through the rest of the house every time you apply a coat or two of varnish or clean your brushes with solvents.

There are plenty of ways to help minimize these sorts of problems. Install a few windows with screens in your workspace to improve fresh air exchange. Attach a dust collector to larger machines and hook a shop vac up to smaller power tools to trap dust and debris close to the source (see page 15). Use an ambient air cleaner with replaceable filters to capture finer dust particles. You might even consider separating your shop from the rest of the basement with a wall and door, which will help control both dust and noise.

A basement workshop with a walk-out entry can be an ideal space for woodworking. Lighting and ventilation are key issues in basements.

Dampness is another relatively common basement problem. High humidity leads to corrosion on metal tools, and lumber can mold or warp if it gets wet. Keep work areas dry by running a dehumidifier during humid months. Buy a hygrometer—a gauge that measures relative humidity—and set it on a shelf or mount it on a wall in the shop where it's easy to see. Try to keep the relative humidity around 40% to help stabilize the moisture content of your lumber. During winter months, you'll probably need to switch from a dehumidifier to a humidifier to keep humidity levels from fluctuating dramatically. (For more on lumber moisture content and how to control it, see Chapter Two.)

Garage shops: In more temperate climates, garages often make better shops than basements. Living spaces stay cleaner when a woodshop is in the garage rather than the basement. Ventilating the shop is as easy as opening the garage door or rolling machinery outside for doing dusty work. Garages usually have high finished ceilings or open trusses, so you can maneuver larger building materials and make taller projects without overhead restrictions. When ceiling or wall framing is exposed, it simplifies the process of running electrical cable for lights and outlets. Plus, you may not have to run the cable through conduit, depending on local building codes. Having a shop on ground level also saves your back from potential straining when you need to move machinery, supplies, and projects in and out of the workshop.

Hygrometers are inexpensive gauges for measuring relative humidity in a room. Keep one in your shop to monitor moisture levels from season to season.

If you'd rather not dedicate your entire garage to a workshop, you can still keep one or more stalls available for parking a car, bicycles, or lawn tractor by simply mounting your tools and workbench on wheels. This way, you can convert the garage into a workshop by backing out vehi-

A garage can easily be converted to a workshop. The garage doors provide instant ventilation, and they allow machinery, lumber, and finished projects to be conveniently moved in and out of the shop.

cles and rolling tools into position, then moving them out of the way when you're finished. You can find rolling bases to fit virtually every kind of woodworking machine, or you can outfit your machines and other shop fixtures with casters mounted on plywood. Wheels make it possible for one person to easily move even the largest machinery.

One problem with most garages is they don't have enough electrical outlets. Those that are present are often fed with an inadequate electrical supply. Many garages, even on new homes, are wired with a single circuit. Some garages on older homes have no electricity all, especially if they are detached from the house. When a garage only serves as parking and storage space, a single electric circuit is sufficient for servicing a garage door opener, an overhead light, and maybe a few light-duty outlets. But once your garage becomes a workshop, you're going to need more electricity to power tools with larger motors, such as table saws and planers (See page 14). Installing new outlets is a relatively inexpensive upgrade, especially if the garage is attached to the house. The wiring work isn't difficult to do if you're comfortable working with electricity, but it should be done in conjunction with a building permit so the work complies with local building codes. If in doubt, hire a qualified electrician.

With ample cross-ventilation, a garage shop is pleasant to work in during spring and fall months, especially if you work in the cool of the day. Winters and summers are a different story, depending on where you live. Garage walls typically aren't insulated, so your workshop can become nearly intolerable to work in on bitterly cold days or during hot, humid summers. Uninsulated spaces will be difficult to heat or cool efficiently. Without a source of heat in the winter, wood glues and finishes won't cure properly below 55°, so you'll have to move gluing and finishing tasks indoors or save them until spring.

Heavy machinery doesn't have to be stationary, thanks to an abundance of rolling base options. They make woodworking possible even in garages that double as parking spaces.

A couple of heating options can make winter woodworking more tolerable and even pleasant. Electric heaters designed for heating a room simply won't generate enough heat to warm an entire garage. Kerosene or propane-fueled heaters, especially those with built-in blowers, will do the job more efficiently. Either choice is safe to use in a garage, provided you open a window or door or raise your garage door a few inches to exhaust carbon monoxide gases. You'll also need to turn off the heater when routing or sawing for long periods of time so the heater flame doesn't ignite the dust. Propane or kerosene is cheaper to use than electricity. It's also more cost-effective than installing a gas furnace or wood-burning stove in your garage, especially if you use the shop only occasionally during the winter.

Cooling a garage shop during the summer can be equally challenging. Cross-ventilation will help draw breezes through the shop, especially if you use a fan to help move the air. If your garage has a window, you might even buy a large room air conditioner. Conditioning the air will bring the temperature down to pleasant working levels as well as remove excess humidity. Insulating the shop will help keep it cool.

Unfinished garage walls make it easy to store supplies, lumber, and tools. Mount shelving, workbenches, lumber racks, and pegboard directly to the wall studs. You can even store lumber and other odds and ends overhead if the roof trusses are accessible, but be careful not to overload these spaces. For sheathed walls, fasten shelving or racks to the wall framing with long deck screws or lag bolts.

Sheds & other outbuildings: Barns and machine sheds present many of the same benefits and drawbacks as garages when it comes to choosing a workshop location. Both barns and sheds offer big doors for unloading supplies and getting fresh air in. You'll have ample space for storing tools and materials as well as lots of open work area. If the floor is hard-packed dirt, it will actually be more forgiving to stand on than concrete for long periods of time. Both types of buildings are difficult to heat in the winter, and you'll probably need to add more lighting as well.

A big garden shed can make a small woodworking shop, but you'll need at least 100 square feet of floor space to get much useful woodworking done. A garden shed can be a good fit if you plan primarily to use hand tools or bench-top-sized machines rather than larger stationary equipment. Most garden sheds aren't wired with electricity, so you'll need to bury a cable from the house to the shed. In smaller sheds, finding enough to room to work might be challenging. One way to expand the workspace is to haul tools outside when the weather permits. Set up a makeshift workbench on a picnic table or a sturdy folding table, or by resting an old door over a couple sawhorses. Small shops—even tiny ones like garden sheds—aren't impossible to work in: they just require creative solutions for maximizing usable space.

Don't let winter leave your unheated shop in the cold. Propane, kerosene, or electric heaters all are options for making workspaces more tolerable.

Building a new shop: Maybe you are one of those lucky folks who have the acreage and finances to erect an outbuilding workshop. If so, you can design the space so it's custom tailored to suit your every need. Adding another building to your property will likely increase your annual property taxes, an issue you won't face by converting a basement or garage stall into a shop. On the other hand, an outbuilding offers you the freedom to partition the workspace and install utilities and insulation without retrofitting or remodeling. Be sure to follow all zoning ordinances that apply to your community when locating the building. Whether you build the shop yourself or hire out the work, apply for the appropriate permits and have the work inspected when necessary during construction. An inspector will need to see the foundation, framing, and wiring when those phases of the job are done. Inspections may seem like a hassle, but they ensure everyone's safety. Skip the building permits and you could be in for costly repairs and fines if the inspector happens to stop by.

Setting up shop

Getting your shop up and running is one thing, but refining it to suit your specific working style will take years. Most woodworkers enjoy the process of creating and recreating a workshop as their tool collections and skills grow. For our purposes, we'll discuss the basics of turning a space into a workshop. Of course you'll need to adapt this general advice to fit your context, budget, and personal preferences. Depending on your space limitations and expectations, the job may be as easy as clearing out some clutter and putting up a workbench.

Estimating how much space you'll need for a shop is difficult to do, particularly if you're just starting out. More than likely, you have a limited amount of room to work with, and you'll use it all. The safe approach is to think big, starting with as much space as you can spare. Shops only get smaller once you add a few pieces of floor-standing machinery or other shop fixtures. Here's a general idea of shop sizes to get you started: For a small shop containing a workbench, lumber storage, and a few full-sized tools, you'll need around 150 square feet of floor space. The space doesn't have to be rectilinear. Even a stretch of basement wall long enough to park your workbench, a few storage shelves, and some tools can provide you with a functional space for building smaller projects.

A single garage stall measures roughly 200 square feet. You can create a flexible, hardworking woodshop in this footprint, especially if you can commit about a third of this space for permanent supply, tool, and fixture storage. Put everything heavy on wheels. Mount lighter things on the walls or ceiling.

Mid-sized home shops containing various large machines will require about 300 square feet of space. In this amount of space, you'll be able to park some machines in one place and leave them there. Anything over 400 square feet is a large shop for a hobbyist woodworker.

Lighting & electrical requirements: It's probably impossible to have too much light in a workshop. Try to have enough light so you won't be forced to work in the shadows. Ideally, workshops should be lit with a combination of overhead and task lighting. Overhead lights illuminate the general workspace, while task lighting directs focused light on the workbench and other machines where you need it most.

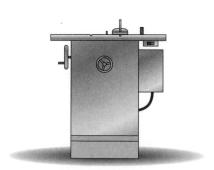

You can illuminate your shop with fluorescent or incandescent light, but the best solution is to use both. Supply general lighting with fluorescents and use incandescents for more direct, task lighting where it's needed.

Ordinary ceiling-mounted incandescent lightbulbs provide reasonable amounts of light in the immediate area under the fixture, but the light drops off quickly, creating shadows. If you prefer the "warm" light produced by lightbulbs, or if your workspace is already outfitted with bulb fixtures, use the highest wattage bulbs they can handle. If you're adding new fixtures, plan for one fixture to illuminate about 16 square feet of floor space. Be sure to install fixtures with protective covers over the bulbs if the shop ceiling is low. Otherwise, sooner or later you'll get a glass shower when you accidentally clip a lightbulb with a long board.

Fluorescent tubes provide more diffuse, even lighting than incandescent lightbulbs. The tubes operate on a fraction of the energy used by incandescent lightbulbs, yet they produce about five times as much light and last about ten times as long.

Fluorescent fixtures come in several sizes and qualities. On the low end, you can buy 4-foot "shop lights" for less than $10 each. However, these budget-priced fixtures have low-quality ballasts that often make an annoying buzzing sound when the lights are on. In colder temperatures, the ballasts warm up slowly and make the bulbs flicker or light dimly. For about two or three times the price of economy fixtures, you can buy better quality 4-foot lights with "industrial" ballasts that start quickly in cold weather. The ballasts operate quietly and outlive their cheaper cousins.

For larger workspaces, consider installing 8-foot fluorescent lighting. Each fixture will cost around $50, which is usually still more economical than buying two premium 4-foot lights. Long fluorescent fixtures are made for commercial applications, so you'll be assured of good-quality ballasts made for cold-weather use. Long fixtures also make for easier installation. You'll only need to hang and wire half as many lights.

If you're installing new shop light fixtures, fluorescent tube lights are the best value. Or, replace incandescent bulbs with screw-in fluorescents if those fixtures are already in place.

The usual criticism of fluorescents is that they cast a surreal greenish or bluish light. This is really only true for two grades of fluorescent bulbs—those sold as "warm white" or "cool white." Actually, several grades of fluorescent bulbs provide more pleasant white light and a truer color spectrum that's closer to natural sunlight. Bulbs rated as "C-50" are a good all-around, mid-priced choice for shop use. Bulbs labeled "CWX" or "Daylight" create light with a color quality even closer to natural light, but they are more expensive.

Task lights are a helpful complement to overhead lighting. Any small bulb fixture can become a task light, provided it can be adjusted easily to direct light right where you need to see. Supplement your general lighting with task lighting whenever the overhead lights create shadows across your work or you need brighter light to see layout lines and other workpiece details. Mount a task light to your workbench, finishing table, and stationary tools. Articulated desk lamps make great workbench task lights, and so do the inexpensive clip-on lights sold for growing indoor plants. Some band saws, drill presses, grinders, and routers come with their own built-in task lights. The extra candlepower shed on these tools really helps.

Tool motor labels will specify how much amperage the machines draw at maximum load. Be sure your shop circuits exceed this limit to keep them from tripping.

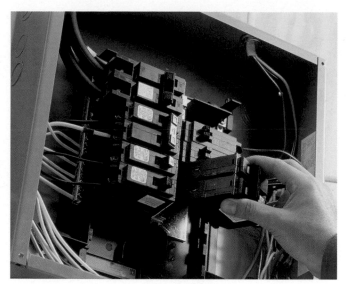

Installing new circuits is not difficult if you have some experience working with electrical systems. If not, call an electrician.

Make the most of natural light if your workspace has windows. Sunlight produces wonderful workshop lighting. A few windows, a skylight, or simply opening garage and service doors can largely supplant artificial lighting during the daytime. Natural light makes even small shops more pleasant to work in while providing you with a healthy dose of vitamin D and some radiant heat. Install skylights so they face north or east if you live in a hot climate. You'll get the benefit of indirect sunlight brightening your space without all the extra heat. For cooler climates, position skylights southward to capture more direct sunlight. Some styles are outfitted with blinds so you can control the amount of light and heat streaming in. You can also cut down UV rays by covering skylights with reflective window film sold at auto parts stores.

Along with ample lighting, you'll need sufficient electricity in your shop. At a minimum, workshops require two circuits. One 15-amp circuit should be dedicated to shop lighting. Otherwise, you could be left in the dark if you trip a circuit breaker while using a machine. The other circuit supplies power for electrical outlets. Read the labels on your tools to identify how many amps they draw at peak loads, then use a circuit rated 20% to 30% over this number. For smaller corded power tools, a 15-amp circuit is usually sufficient. Full-sized table saws, planers, jointers, and dust collectors should draw power from a 20-amp circuit. Large tools that produce 2 hp or more are generally wired for 220-volt operation, which requires at least a 30-amp circuit. If you'll be running an air-conditioner or large electric heater in the shop, these appliances should have dedicated circuits, too.

Check your home's main electric service panel to see how many circuit slots are still open. If you don't have room to add two or more new circuits for the shop, a licensed electrician can install a smaller panel of additional circuit breakers, called a *subpanel*. Subpanels are also useful when your shop is located in the garage far from the main service panel. Having a subpanel in the shop allows you to switch circuits on and off conveniently without trudging all the way to the main panel.

CAUTION: Adding new circuits to the main service panel may exceed its amperage capacity, even if there are slots available for more circuits. This all depends on how many other large appliances are drawing power from the panel. An electrician can determine whether adding more circuits or a subpanel will be safe for your current main panel. If adding new circuits will exceed the panel's amperage capacity, the solution is to install a larger 100- or 200-amp main panel and possibly larger main service drops from the utility pole. These are expensive but essential upgrades.

Use heavy-gauge extension cords in the shortest usable lengths to power your tools. This cord will be adequate for tools drawing 15 amps or less, provided it's not overly long.

Garages and basements typically don't have enough outlets to accommodate a full workshop. Single outlets are easy to expand by plugging in a power strip. If possible, position your workbench close to an outlet and mount the power strip right on your bench. You'll be able to plug in a number of power tools or battery chargers at once, provided all these tools and devices aren't used simultaneously.

Clear the air and keep your shop cleaner with one or more dust-collection devices. Dedicated dust collectors, ambient air cleaners and shop vacs are all options.

The larger difficulty of having too few outlets is that you'll have to use extension cords to deliver power where it's needed or move machines around the shop in order to plug them in. Extension cords can be used safely to power most tools provided the cord's amperage rating is greater than the tool's peak amperage draw. In other words, if the tool draws 12 amps under maximum load, use an extension cord rated for 15 or more amps. (See your owner's manual or a sticker on the tool motor to check the tool's amperage requirements.) Whenever you need an extension cord, use the shortest cord length possible. As the cord length increases, the wires inside develop more resistance to electrical flow and their amperage capacity drops. If a cord is too long, it can starve a tool of optimal power, which leads to more heat build up in both the cord and the tool. Tool motors will wear prematurely under these conditions. A better solution to using extension cords is to add more outlets in your shop. Plan for several outlets on each wall. Ideally, install one outlet every 6 feet.

NOTE: If you wire your shop yourself rather than hire out this work, be aware that local building codes may require all exposed wiring be contained in rigid metal or PVC conduit unless it can be stapled firmly to wall and ceiling framing. Codes may also dictate that wall receptacles be ground-fault protected. Call your local building inspector to review the codes that will impact your shop wiring project.

Air quality & ventilation: Sawdust and fumes from stains, varnishes, and other finishing supplies can compromise the air quality in your shop. Contaminated air isn't just unpleasant to breathe, it's unhealthy. The verdict is still out on the long-term health consequences of breathing wood dust, but play it safe by providing plenty of fresh air in your shop. Use portable fans to move the air through windows and doors when you are sanding, sawing, or routing. Place the fan in a window or doorway opposite another open window or door to create a cross breeze. When your woodworking tool arsenal grows large enough to include those really dusty tools, especially table saws, stationary sanders, and planers, you may want to invest in a dedicated dust collector to capture dust, wood chips, and other debris right at the source. Dust collectors with hoses that connect to tools won't purify the surrounding air in your shop, but you

Probably the greatest asset of a workbench is how it brings work up to a comfortable height and keeps you from stooping.

Cabinetmaker's benches are usually outfitted with end vises and bench dogs for holding workpieces securely.

can keep your lungs cleaner by wearing a dust respirator or installing an ambient air cleaner with replaceable filters.

Workbenches: Workbenches are fundamental shop fixtures that help you work at a comfortable height. They hold project parts securely while you work on them and keep tools and supplies within easy reach. If you don't have one yet, put it near the top of your list of projects to build, or buy a prefabricated bench. Woodworking supply catalogs and home centers sell workbenches, but you can probably build a bench of equal or better quality yourself for less than what you'll pay for a ready-made bench. Project books often include plans for workbenches, and woodworking magazines publish workbench stories nearly every year.

Benches fall into three broad categories: traditional cabinetmaker's benches, utility workbenches, and collapsible/portable styles. Traditional benches are those with thick hardwood tops and sturdy wooden leg bases. They're free-standing, so you can position them wherever you need to and work around all four sides. Bench dimensions are typically 2 feet wide and 4 to 6 feet long. The top worksurface tends to be a laminated blank of hard maple, beech, or other hardwood. The extra thickness helps absorb vibrations produced by heavy pounding, and the added weight keeps the bench stationary. Benchtops are often outfitted with a series of holes along one long edge or at the end. Wood or metal pegs, called bench dogs, fit into these holes and work in conjunction with a vise on the bench to hold long boards or large workpieces.

Traditional benches will have at least one large metal vise; many have two, with one on the side and one on an end. Better vises have a "quick-release" feature for sliding the jaws open and closed, a heavy screw or chain drive mechanism, and a stout handle. Some have a pop-up bench dog on the top. Vise jaws should be lined with wood faces to keep the metal jaws from marring soft workpieces. Depending on the bench style, there may be a recessed tray in the top for holding hand tools as well as a shelf underneath. If you buy a traditional bench, expect to pay more than $500 for a good one.

Utility workbenches are easy to build and a good value for woodworking and general home improvement tasks. The benches may resemble cabinetmaker styles with a heavy top and a skeletal base, or they can be as simple as a sheet of plywood on top of a closed cabinet or two. A utility workbench can be free-standing, or you can fasten it to wall studs. Your bench will be more useful with a vise, but you can often forego the vise and use C-clamps or other short clamps to secure your work to the benchtop. Another option is to buy a clamp-on vise and fix it to the benchtop only when you need it.

If you're organizing your shop on a tight budget, you can build a sturdy work-bench using framing lumber and plywood for less than $100. Double-up 2 × 4s to make the legs, and design the bench with a sturdy framework of 2 × 4s under the top to keep it flat. Make the top with two layers of ¾-inch plywood, or use heav-ier medium-density fiberboard (commonly called MDF). MDF is extremely dense and flat, and has a smooth surface that won't splinter. It's also quite economical and resists wear and tear, especially if you protect the edges with strips of hard-wood. Install a shelf or two below your bench. Use this storage area for organiz-ing tool cases, extra lumber, or other items you reach for regularly in your work.

Depending on your storage and project needs, you can outfit the space under your workbench top with open shelving, closed cabinets, or a combination of both. If floor-space is in short supply, buy a collapsible workbench and fold it up for storage.

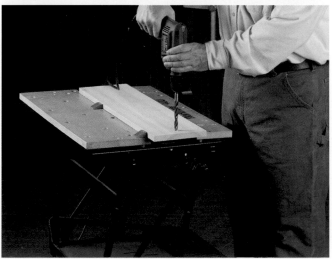

Size the bench proportions so you can work comfortably while standing and still reach across the top from one side. For average-sized people, 30 to 40 inches is a good working height. Large benchtops are handy for holding both your project and the tools you're using at the moment, but deep storage areas under them can become black holes for misplacing tools. It's also difficult to size up your spare lumber supply if you store stacks of it under a monstrous bench. Keep the bench width to 3 feet or less and the length not more than about 8 feet.

One way to add flexibility to your floorspace is to mount your workbench on casters. Buy heavy-duty casters made to support at least 100 pounds each, and make sure two of the four casters have brakes to park the bench during use. Larger diameter wheels will make a bench easier to roll around. Another space-saving option is to design your bench so it mounts to a wall and flips up when not in use. Attach the bench to the wall with four to six large door hinges screwed to a ledger board that's bolted to the wall studs.

Sawhorses make handy supplemental worksurfaces for cutting or assembly tasks. Plastic or metal sawhorses are lightweight and collapsible, or make your own inexpensive sawhorses from scrap wood.

Portable workbenches are economical and versatile alternatives to larger, permanent benches. They make great companions to your full-sized workbench, but they probably won't meet all your bench needs. Most styles have a worksurface that opens and closes like a clamp. The metal base folds up for convenient storage. Portable workbenches make stable outfeed tables for supporting workpieces as they leave your table saw or planer. Their wide stance keeps them from tipping over or shifting like other lightweight roller stands do. Clamp a large piece of plywood in the top vise to create a broader surface for project assembly, staging parts, or doing light machine work. Simply fasten a cleat to the plywood and tighten the benchtop clamp onto this cleat.

Sawhorses serve as portable workbenches too. Whether you buy or build yours, have a pair in the shop to provide extra worksurfaces for assembly or for small power tool use. Metal or plastic styles are lightweight, sturdy, and inexpensive. Many fold up so you can tuck them out of the way. If you build your sawhorses, experiment with their height to see what works best. Some woodworkers prefer shorter sawhorses for supporting larger projects. Keep the overall height to 3 feet or less.

Material storage: Organizing the various sundries and tools in your shop will require several types of storage. Narrow shelving works well for storing spare lumber, bins of fasteners, containers of finishing materials, and smaller power tools. Drawers, provided they aren't too deep or large, work well for organizing loose articles that don't stand on their own, stack well, or fit into uniform-

Ample storage is an important component of a workshop. This shop features drawers and shelves for storing and organizing tools and materials.

ly sized containers. Locking drawers keep sharp blades and bits out of children's hands and store smaller, valuable shop tools securely. Mechanic's multi-drawer tool carts are particularly useful shop fixtures, because they offer a bank of sturdy drawers in various depths as well as a bit of flat workspace on top, all on wheels.

You'll also need a container for collecting smaller pieces of scrap lumber or for tossing cutoffs as you make them. A spare trash can works reasonably well for this purpose. Resist the urge to save every scrap. Keep your scrap bin small and cull it from time to time.

Plywood and other large sheet materials are best stored flat on their faces, but it's tough to do this in a small shop. To help keep plywood flat, store it on edge against a wall and strap it to the wall framing. Or build a narrow plywood storage cart that holds the sheets at a slight angle so gravity helps keep them flat and stacked neatly. Plywood storage carts are relatively common building projects. You'll see designs for them in woodworking magazines from time to time.

Wall-mounted lumber storage racks keep lumber off the floor and out of your way. Racks ensure the lumber stays flat until you're ready to use it.

Pegboard is a thrifty way to hang hand tools near the workbench. Fasten furring strips or other scrap material to the back of the pegboard to form a shallow framework, then screw the pegboard to wall studs. Furring strips hold pegboard off the wall so metal pegboard hooks have room to slip into the holes. Buy hooks made to stay in the holes, or you'll discover that they have an annoying tendency to fall out and get lost.

Store pipe and bar clamps by hanging them from cleats or thick dowel pegs mounted to the wall. C-clamps and spring clamps hang conveniently from pegs, or you can slip a length of rope through them, tie loops on the ends of the rope, and hang the clamps from nails. Clamp carts are another option for keeping these tools neatly arranged. Usually a clamp cart will be designed to hold all sorts of clamps. Casters make the cart easy to roll close to your bench or wherever you're assembling a project.

Tooling up: You'll learn in subsequent chapters that most woodworking tasks can be accomplished in more than one way using different tools. For a begin-

A dedicated clamp rack holds clamps in a single location, helping you maintain a well organized shop.

ner, this means you can explore many techniques without owning a shop full of tools. On the flip side, if your tool collection is modest, some tasks may be more challenging to tackle without the optimal tool. Arguably, the best reason for owning lots of different tools is that it gives you more options for working efficiently and accurately. For instance, you can learn to plane board faces flat

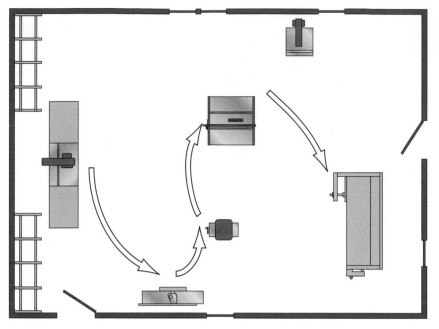

A well organized shop has a logical order of machinery, with the table saw placed in the center and the lumber stored conveniently near the door.

with a hand plane, but an electric surface planer can turn a planing task into a five-minute job with virtually no learning curve. A jig saw cuts decent curves, but a band saw cuts them cleaner and in a wider range of material thicknesses.

The particular tools you buy and the time it takes you to master them influence how you progress as a skillfull woodworker. There isn't an ideal shopping list for what tools to own as a beginner. In reality, you'll get accustomed to using whatever you buy and become increasingly proficient with them the more you practice. At some point in time, you may actually own all the tools you really need for the type of woodworking you do and the projects you like to build. On the other hand, you may enjoy the variety and challenge of learning new techniques and mastering new tools. Your tool arsenal may be constantly growing and evolving.

Generally speaking, most woodworking tasks are easier to learn and faster to carry out successfully with power tools, especially for novices. This is why more emphasis is placed on power tools than hand tools in this book.

Shop layout: Arranging tools, materials, and fixtures in your shop will depend on the shape of the space you have, where doors, windows, stairwells, and outlets are located, and the size and mobility of the machinery you own. Here are some general guidelines to start with when laying out your shop: Locate shelves or racks for storing lumber or sheet goods close to entry doors and stairwells. This way, you'll carry them the shortest distance into the shop. If you own a power miter saw, situate it close to these raw materials so you can size them down before moving them to other places in the shop. Depending on the amount of lumber you plan to have on hand, you may even be able to mount your miter saw above or below your lumber rack where it will be most convenient for processing the wood.

It's likely that you'll use a table saw for making some of the first cuts on lumber and sheet goods after they enter the shop. Table saws require 4 to 8 feet of clear space all around so there's room to work without hitting walls or other obstructions. Place the saw near the center of the shop and leave it there, if you can. Keep the thickness planer and jointer near the table saw for the same reason. These three tools are the real workhorses of lumber processing. If you're working with roughsawn lumber, generally you'll need to run long boards through the jointer and planer before cutting them up. Turning a board into parts may require you to go from planer to jointer to table saw and back to the jointer or planer again. The closer these machines are to one another, the less walking you'll need to do to switch from one operation to the next.

Try to establish some flat workspace nearby for staging workpieces temporarily as they leave the saw, jointer, or planer. Your workbench could serve this purpose, especially if the bench height is the same height as the table saw or a bit shorter. This way, the bench won't interfere with oversized workpieces as you cut them on the table saw. You may even be able to use your workbench as a support surface for the table saw during ripping or crosscutting.

Arrange other machines and shop fixtures where they are convenient for you. Have a bin near the miter saw for collecting short scraps. Place a stationary sander near a window to draw out the airborne dust. Router tables and band saws can be stored anywhere, provided they are on wheels. A drill press should stand against a wall where it's less likely to tip over. Keep measuring and marking tools, hand tools, containers of fasteners, and glue close to the workbench. Above all, lay out your workspace to minimize duplication of effort and allow you to move easily and safely from one area to the next.

Safety overview

Shop accidents happen in an instant, especially with power tools. The results can be irreversible and even life-threatening. Your first line of defense against mishaps is really simple: Think before acting. Respect the capabilities and dangers of your tools and know how to use them safely. Plan your work so you can get help lifting or moving heavy articles. Set high standards for tool maintenance and operation. Never use dull blades and bits. Remove guards and other safety devices only when absolutely necessary. Keep the workspace clean and the floor clear of debris so you can avoid stepping in or over scraps and piles of shavings. Consider your shop to be an extension of your own character and a reflection of good work habits.

Personal safety gear will help you avoid accidents and work comfortably. Virtually every task that requires a tool creates some degree of danger for your eyes. Buy safety glasses or goggles that fit your face properly and have an anti-fog coating. They should protect your eyes from both the front and sides. Prescription glasses shouldn't be used in place of safety glasses. Find safety goggles that fit over your prescription glasses instead. Put on your safety eyewear as soon as you enter the shop, regardless of what woodworking you plan to do. Keep them clean and protected against scratches when not in use. If the glasses offer you a clear view of what you're doing and feel natural once they're on, you're more likely to wear them. After a while, it will feel strange working without them.

Wood dust is irritating to breathe and probably harmful to your health over the long haul. Wear a disposable respirator or one with replaceable filters to protect your lungs.

Power tool use can be equally damaging to your ears. Safety gear manufacturers offer a variety of different ear protection devices to suit personal preference. You'll find ear muffs that cover your ears and earplugs that fit inside. Some plugs are disposable and made of soft foam that you compress and insert in your ear canals. Once inside, the foam expands for a tight seal. Other earplug styles are reusable and outfitted on bands or cords for wearing around your neck. You'll even find combination head gear with safety glasses mounted on ear muffs. Whatever style of hearing protection you choose, be sure it has a noise reduction rating (NRR) of at least 25 decibels, which is a safe standard for general power tool use. Wear your ear protection whenever you use a motorized tool, not just the loudest ones.

Research now suggests that wood dust can be a carcinogen, as well as an irritant. When you are using dust-producing machinery, especially saws, routers and sanders, wear a respirator. Respirators approved for wood dusts are different than inexpensive "hospital style" masks, although they look similar to one another. Usually, dust respirators will have two head straps rather than one, and the packaging will clearly identify the product as a respirator and not a dust mask. Dust masks actually offer little protection from fine wood dust. If you are working with solvent- or oil-based strippers, cleaners, or finishes, a dust respirator will not filter out the mists and fumes produced by these materials. Wear a respirator outfitted with replaceable canister filters, and change the filters as soon as you can smell solvents through the mask.

Your arsenal of safety gear should include both hearing and eye protection. Buy comfortable styles so you'll wear them willingly whenever you're using machinery.

As for other apparel, roll up long shirt sleeves to keep them clear of machinery and messes. Wear comfortable shoes with rubber soles if you'll be standing for long periods of time. Athletic shoes are a great choice for woodworking wear. Dress warmly if you work in an unheated shop, but avoid wearing gloves when using power tools. Gloves can get caught on blades or bits and pull your hands into harm's way. Some woodworkers wear aprons while they work to keep clothes cleaner. If you do, be sure to empty the pockets of loose articles and the apron strings.

Create a safety area in your shop with a first-aid kit and a fire extinguisher rated for both chemical and electrical fires. Place these items near the door or stairwell so you

Keep a first-aid kit, fire extinguisher, and phone in a convenient location near the shop exit.

TOOLS BY TASK

The following groupings of tools are not intended to be an exhaustive list, nor should you feel obligated to have every tool in each group. If you're just starting out, use these tool groupings as suggestions for what to buy or borrow. Watch for tools such as routers and table saws that appear in multiple groups. Their versatility provides the best value for your tool dollars.

Preparing stock
- Thickness planer (12-13 inches)
- Jointer (6-inch)
  Hand planes (jointer, jack, block)

Measuring, marking, & layout
- Combination square
- Try square
- Framing square
- Bevel gauge
- Tape measure (25-feet)
- Compass
  Chalk line

Ripping, crosscutting, cutting angles
- Table saw
- Power miter saw
- Circular saw
  Band saw
  Jig saw

Cutting curves, cutouts, template work
- Jig saw
- Router
- Band saw
  Scroll saw
  Reciprocating saw

Drilling holes
  Corded drill
- Cordless drill/driver
  Drill press

Forming wood joints
- Table saw
- Router
- Router table w/ fence
  Dovetailing jig
  Biscuit joiner
  Mortising machine
  Drill press with mortising attachment
- Block plane (low-angle)
- Rabbeting plane
- Chisels

Shaping, carving wood
- Router
- Lathe
  Rotary carving tool
  Carving knives
  Chisels
  Mallet (wooden or brass head)
  Block plane (low-angle)
- Files, rasps
  Spokeshave

Sanding, smoothing, scraping
- Belt sander
- Random-orbit sander
- ¼-sheet pad sander
- Drill press with sanding drum attachments
  Stationary disk sander
- Stationary disk/belt sander
  Oscillating spindle sander

  Wide-belt sander
  Cabinet scraper
  Hand planes (jointer, jack, block)
  Paint scraper

Driving/removing fasteners
- Hammers (framing, tack)
- Nail sets
- Screwdrivers
- Cordless drill/driver
- Wrenches, sockets
  Pneumatic nail guns
- Pliers or nail puller
- Short pry bar or cat's paw

Clamping & assembly
- C-clamps
- Long pipe or bar clamps (3-, 6-, 8-feet)
- Short bar clamps 18-, 24-inch)
  Spring clamps
  Hand screws
- Bench vise
  Mallets (deadblow, rubber, wooden head)

Sharpening tool blades
- Water, oil or diamond-impregnated stones
- Angle-setting jig
  Low-speed grinder

- = Preferred tool or tools for the task

can reach them on the way out of the shop in the event of an emergency. It's also a good idea to have a phone in the shop at all times.

If you work alone in the shop, plan your woodworking sessions when someone else is home and can check on you from time to time or lend a hand if necessary. To avoid accidents and mistakes, stop working if you are feeling tired, frustrated, or rushed. It should go without saying that it's never safe to operate woodworking machinery when you're under the influence of alcohol or other drugs that impair your judgment.

Throughout this book, look for cautionary reminders printed in italic type. Be sure you understand the warning before proceeding.

Chapter 2
WOOD BASICS

For many woodworkers, the experience of selecting and buying lumber is just as exciting as unpacking a long-awaited new tool. There's something gratifying about driving to the lumberyard with list in hand, then rummaging through the stacks for the best boards. The fragrance of freshly sawn wood, the whine of a saw somewhere in the background, and aisles upon aisles of wood-working supplies really bolster the creative spirit. Once you've got that fresh stack of lumber home, waiting until you have time to commit it to a project will surely test your patience.

In the midst of all the excitement, it's important to choose lumber thoughtfully. First, become familiar with the species of lumber available at your local home center or lumberyard. Most lumber retailers will stock at least a half dozen different species, and the options can vary from region to region. Some lumber types will be appropriate for your project, while others will not. For instance, lumber intended for outdoor projects typically won't be the right choice for making a jewelry box or end table. You won't find a list of the best uses on the lumber rack tag, so it's up to you to know your woods. Better lumberyards will offer several grades of the same species, sometimes in limited sizes and with varying degrees of surfacing already done for you. Picking what's best for your application will also depend on the tools you have to use, the limits of your budget, and even your skill level, to some degree. This chapter will help sort through these kinds of issues.

There are many sources for buying lumber besides the closest lumberyard. Private sawmills, mail-order catalogs, classified ads in the newspaper, and on-line auctions are other possibilities. Lumberyards and mail-order suppliers sell wood differently than home centers, and these distinctions can be confusing. On-line lumber auctions may help you nab the best price per board, but other costs and issues involved with buying lumber sight unseen may make your actual savings a wash. Each supplier offers certain benefits and poses some drawbacks to a hobbyist woodworker. We'll cover the basics later in the chapter. Knowing your supplier options can save you money and minimize unpleasant surprises.

Once you've made your purchase, you should know how to store it appropriately until you need it, then how to flatten and smooth it properly. We'll cover storage and surfacing techniques in the pages to follow. Finally, this chapter will provide an overview of what to know when selecting and buying sheet goods such as plywood and particleboard. In certain situations, sheet materials are better choices than board lumber for project parts.

Hardwoods vs. softwoods

Lumber can be grouped into two broad categories—hardwoods and softwoods—based on a botanical distinction. Hardwoods are those species that come from deciduous, or leaf-bearing trees that produce fruits, flowers, or nuts. Common North American hardwood lumber includes oak, maple, cherry, ash, walnut, beech, birch, and poplar. There are many less common Western hardwoods as well, including butternut, mesquite, pear, holly, and sycamore. Other countries log innumerable hardwood species, too. Some of these exotics include teak, cocobolo, mahogany, ebony, rosewood, purpleheart, and bubinga. You can find them through mail-order houses or specialty lumberyards. Most are expensive and may be available only in limited sizes.

Softwoods come from conifers—the large family of cone-bearing trees that bear needles rather than leaves. Pines and firs of many sorts, redwood, cypress, and cedar are typical North American softwoods made into board lumber. Because these species are well suited for construction purposes, all lumber used for framing and rough construction comes from softwood trees. They're sufficiently strong for structural applications, yet still are easy to work with common hand or power tools. Another advantage is that conifers grow rapidly and develop straighter trunks and branches than deciduous trees. Finally, more softwood trees can be planted per acre than hardwood trees, so they produce a higher lumber yield in less time.

Lumber can be divided into two botanical categories: softwoods and hardwoods. Softwood lumber comes from coniferous, or cone-bearing, trees. Hardwood lumber comes from broad-leafed trees that produce fruits, flowers, or nuts.

It's a common misconception that hardwoods are called hardwoods because the wood is hard, while softwoods are soft. It's true that many hardwoods are more difficult to machine than softwoods, but the distinction actually has nothing to do with hardness or workability. Southern yellow pine, for instance, is a heavy, dense softwood used for stair treads and large framing lumber. It machines and accepts fasteners in a manner like that of hardwood. Walnut and poplar are common hardwoods, but they can be routed and sawn as easily as cedar or redwood. Even pricing isn't a good indicator of hardwoods or softwoods. More softwood is manufactured into building materials than furniture-grade lumber, but what does become lumber can be quite expensive. For example, clear sugar pine lumber is just as costly as premium cherry or white oak. Actually, the basic economics of supply and demand have more to do with lumber pricing than the particular species of wood or even its grade designation.

Choosing what to use

Both hardwoods and softwoods can be used for woodworking projects. Generally, hardwoods end up as indoor furniture, cabinetry, turnings, and trimwork because the wood grain and figure are highly desirable. Softwoods tend to become outdoor furniture, children's projects, and other sorts of utility or painted projects. These are merely general guidelines. If money is no object, you can build children's furniture from practically any furniture-grade lumber you like.

So what species should you choose for a particular project? The answer isn't cut and dried, and generally you'll have more than one good option. To help pare down your choices, here are a few questions to ask yourself:

Is this an indoor or outdoor project? Most woods will degrade over time in the presence of water or ultraviolet sunlight. Moisture breaks wood down much faster than does sunlight. Damp wood invites mold growth and wood-boring insects, especially if it's kept in a cool, dark place or in contact with the ground. Sunlight bleaches wood color, and the UV rays both dry the lumber and weaken its cellular structure. If you're building outdoor furniture or other yard and garden projects, some of the durable outdoor woods include western red cedar, redwood, cypress, and white oak. These woods contain natural oils or pore-filling compounds that resist rot and help repel insects. Boatbuilding woods such as teak and mahogany are excellent choices as well, but they are much more expensive than the common weather-resistant species.

If you're building an outdoor project that won't come in contact with food or skin, consider using pressure-treated lumber. It takes paint well once the infused chemicals dry, and the wood tends to be warranted for decades against rotting. Wear a dust respirator when machining pressure-treated lumber to keep from inhaling the sawdust, which contains the treating chemicals. Dispose of the scraps in the trash rather than burning them. The chemical formulations create harmful fumes when they're burned, and to do so is illegal.

Will the project be painted or receive a clear finish? For painted projects, choose lumber that has a smooth texture without a heavy grain pattern. Ideally, the lumber should sand and finish so smoothly that the grain entirely disappears. Good paint-grade hardwoods include poplar, birch, and aspen. These also tend to be less expensive than hardwoods with more attractive wood grain patterns. Softwoods generally produce a blotchy, uneven tone when they're finished with stain, but they make excellent, economical painted woods. Pines, firs, and other "white woods" are good candidates for paint finishes. Avoid using cedar for indoor painted projects. The natural oil in cedar can bleed through a

ASH

Origin: Southeastern United States
Properties: Straight-grained with coarse texture. Shock-resistant. Moderately heavy and hard.
Workability/Finishing: Takes fasteners, glue and finishes well. Excellent for steam-bending and turning.
Uses: Tool handles, baseball bats, general furniture construction, veneer.
Price: Inexpensive

MAPLE (HARD)

Origin: Northeastern United States and Canada
Properties: Dense, with straight, curly, or wavy grain patterns and good figure.
Workability/Finishing: Can dull steel blades and bits. Predrill before installing screws or nails. Uneven grain pattern can produce blotching with stain finishes.
Uses: Flooring, butcher block and cutting boards, general furniture construction, veneer.
Price: Moderate to expensive, depending on figure

ASPEN

Origin: United States and Canada
Properties: Tight-grained and moderately hard.
Workability/Finishing: Takes routed profiles, fasteners, glues, and painted finishes well. Stained finishes produce blotchy, uneven appearance.
Uses: Good secondary wood for furniture construction.
Price: Inexpensive

POPLAR

Origin: Northern Canada and Alaska
Properties: Moderately hard with fine grain pattern and varied color.
Workability/Finishing: Works easily with steel blades and bits. Takes paint finishes well, but stains will produce blotching.
Uses: Good secondary wood for furniture construction, toys, shop jigs, pallets, and crates.
Price: Inexpensive

BIRCH (YELLOW)

Origin: Northeastern United States
Properties: Straight-grained with even texture. Dense and heavy.
Workability/Finishing: Easily worked with both hand and power tools. Good for turning and steam-bending. Takes glue and clear finishes well.
Uses: General furniture construction, veneer, shop jigs.
Price: Inexpensive to moderate

RED OAK

Origin: Eastern United States and Canada
Properties: Varied density and grain pattern, from straight to slight figure. Large open pore structure on end grain.
Workability/Finishing: Works easily with sharp steel or carbide blades and bits. Takes fasteners, glue, and stain finishes well. Coarse texture can lead to splintering.
Uses: General furniture construction, veneer, flooring.
Price: Moderate

CHERRY

Origin: Eastern and Southern United States
Properties: Even to figured grain pattern and moderately hard. Warpage common during drying. Good steam-bending properties.
Workability/Finishing: Excellent working characteristics with hand or power tools. Takes finishes well.
Uses: General furniture construction, turning, veneer.
Price: Moderate

WALNUT

Origin: Eastern United States and Canada, Central and South America
Properties: Moderately soft and dense with varied grain pattern and color.
Workability/Finishing: Works easily with hand and power tools. Good for turning. Exceptional for clear finishes.
Uses: General furniture construction, gun stocks, musical instruments, carving and turning, veneer.
Price: Moderate to expensive

HICKORY

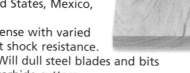

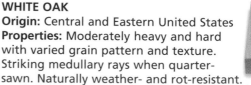
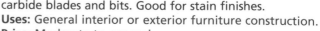

Origin: Southern United States, Mexico, and Central America
Properties: Hard and dense with varied grain pattern. Excellent shock resistance.
Workability/Finishing: Will dull steel blades and bits quickly. Machine with carbide cutters.
Uses: Tool handles, sporting equipment, veneer, furniture construction.
Price: Moderate where regionally plentiful

WHITE OAK

Origin: Central and Eastern United States
Properties: Moderately heavy and hard with varied grain pattern and texture. Striking medullary rays when quartersawn. Naturally weather- and rot-resistant.
Workability/Finishing: Works easily with sharp steel or carbide blades and bits. Good for stain finishes.
Uses: General interior or exterior furniture construction.
Price: Moderate to expensive

AROMATIC CEDAR

Origin: Eastern United States and Canada
Properties: Soft with variable grain pattern and texture. Emits distinct aroma that deters moths.
Workability/Finishing: Works easily with hand or power tools. Takes glues and clear finishes well, but fasteners should be coated or stainless to prevent corrosion.
Uses: Closet and chest linings, veneer, turning, paneling.
Price: Inexpensive

CEDAR (WESTERN RED)

Origin: Pacific Northwest into Canada
Properties: Soft, straight-grained with coarse texture. Lightweight. Naturally weather- and insect-resistant.
Workability/Finishing: Similar working properties to aromatic cedar. Can be stained, primed and painted, or left unfinished and allowed to weather to a silvery gray.
Uses: Exterior furniture, arbors, decks, fences.
Price: Inexpensive

CYPRESS

Origin: Southern United States
Properties: Soft, straight-grained and lightweight. Naturally weather- and insect-resistant.
Workability/Finishing: Works easily with hand and power tools. Accepts glue, fasteners, paints, and stains well.
Uses: Exterior furniture, boatbuilding, trimwork, beams.
Price: Inexpensive where regionally plentiful

REDWOOD (SEQUOIA)

Origin: Western United States into Pacific Northwest
Properties: Soft, even-grained with varied coloration. Naturally weather- and insect-resistant.
Workability/Finishing: Works easily with hand and power tools. Accepts glue, fasteners, stains, and paints well.
Uses: Exterior furniture, structures, siding, decks, fences.
Price: Expensive

WHITE PINE (WESTERN)

Origin: Western United States and Canada
Properties: Soft with straight-grained, uniform texture.
Workability/Finishing: Works easily with hand and power tools. Accepts glue, fasteners, and paints well.
Uses: General furniture construction, millwork, veneer.
Price: Moderate

MAHOGANY (AMERICAN)

Origin: Central and South America
Properties: Medium density with straight, interlocked or irregular grain pattern that produces striking figure. Naturally weather-resistant.
Workability/Finishing: Ideal for hand tool work as well as machining. Accepts fasteners, glue, and finishes well.
Uses: General furniture construction, carving, boatbuilding, turning, veneer.
Price: Moderate to expensive

PADAUK (AFRICAN)

Origin: West Africa
Properties: Straight to interlocked grain. Texture varies from moderate to coarse. Naturally weather-resistant.
Workability/Finishing: Easily worked with sharp steel or carbide blades and bits. Excellent carving and turning wood.
Uses: Furniture construction, carving, turning, veneer.
Price: Moderate to expensive

ROSEWOOD (INDIAN)

Origin: Southern India
Properties: Even texture, dense and heavy. Decorative grain pattern.
Workability/Finishing: Dulls steel blades and hand tools quickly, so carbide cutters are recommended. Difficult to join with fasteners.
Uses: Inlay, turnings, carving, musical instruments, boatbuilding, veneer.
Price: Expensive

TEAK

Origin: Central America, Southeast Asia
Properties: Hard, dense, heavy, and evenly textured. High oil content makes teak naturally weather-resistant. Wood dust can be a respiratory irritant.
Workability/Finishing: Hardness makes teak difficult to machine. Use carbide blades and bits. Accepts glue and stain well, but predrill before installing fasteners.
Uses: Interior and exterior furniture, boatbuilding.
Price: Expensive

ZEBRAWOOD

Origin: West Africa
Properties: Hard, interlocked grain pattern with light-and-dark varigated grain pattern.
Workability/Finishing: Will dull steel bits and blades, so carbide cutters are recommended.
Uses: Turning, inlay, decorative veneer, furniture.
Price: Expensive

Cedar must be covered with a stain-sealing primer before it is painted, or natural oils will bleed through the paint and leave brown stains.

painted finish, leaving brown streaks. Another good option for painted projects is to build them from sheet material such as medium-density fiberboard (See page 41) instead of solid wood.

If you plan to finish your project with stain and a transparent topcoat, the best wood choices are those that accept stain evenly without blotching. Oak is a good all-around candidate for stain, but cherry, maple, and pine often absorb stain unevenly. Sometimes the only way to know how a wood will accept stain is to test the finish on a sample piece. For more on coloring wood with stains, dyes, or other transparent finishes, see chapter 6.

What thicknesses and proportions of lumber does your project require? Virtually all the board lumber you'll find at a home center or general-purpose lumberyard will be milled to ¾-inch thickness. There may be a small display of "craft" lumbers in ¼- and ½-inch thicknesses made of oak or poplar as well as laminated blanks in a few sizes up to 3 inches thick. Lengths of craft lumber will be limited to about 3 feet. If you need thin lumber in larger sizes, some specialty yards will plane down thicker stock for a nominal planing fee. Or find another woodworker with a surface planer to plane down your wood. For lumber thicker than ¾ inch, shop at a lumberyard that specializes in furniture lumbers (see page 37), or glue several ¾-inch-thick pieces together and plane down the lamination to whatever thickness you need.

Sometimes projects require large panels. Tables and entertainment centers are good examples. If you don't own a jointer and clamps to glue your own wide panels from narrower boards, your local home center probably stocks pre-glued, sanded panels as wide as 3 feet and up to 8 feet long. The selection will be limited to just a few species, usually oak, pine, aspen, and maple. Occasionally you can substitute plywood for a solid-wood panel, then cover the edges with veneer edge tape or strips of solid wood. If none of these options will do, you'll have to glue up your own panel from individual boards (see page 115).

Notice how the oak sample (left in photo) absorbs stain more evenly than the maple sample (right in photo), which absorbs more stain in some areas than others. If you plan to stain a project, choose your wood species carefully with the finish in mind.

Which project parts show? A common practice in furniture building is to reserve the most attractive wood for those parts that show: drawer faces, aprons, tabletops, doors, legs, and so forth. If your project includes parts that won't show or are usually concealed, consider buying less expensive wood and using it here. Poplar and pine are often integrated into projects made from more expensive hardwoods to serve as "secondary" woods for drawer sides and bottoms, internal framework, and back panels. Here's a good way to save money without compromising function or durability.

What does the budget dictate? Lumber is expensive, particularly if you buy it completely surfaced. Sometimes sticker shock will push you over the edge and make your choice of lumber obvious. When tallying up the amount of lumber you'll need, factor in another 20% to 30% more wood. The overage invariably gets used in the end. If the price is out of reach, consider using a more economical lumber and staining it to match the color of a costlier wood. Sometimes you can substitute a species that mimics a more expensive alternative. Alder, for example, is much more economical than Honduras mahogany, but the two woods look surprisingly similar.

How do your tools and skills impact wood choice? Some woods are easier to work with than others. Resist the urge to buy exotics or even hardwoods for those first few projects. As lovely as they are, exotics are expensive, and many are difficult to cut, drill, and fasten together. Some present special gluing and finishing hassles too. Same story goes for domestic hardwoods such as oak, maple, ash, and beech. While it's certainly possible to work these woods with a portable drill and circular saw, the tasks are much easier with a drill press and table saw. Softwoods such as pine or cedar are more forgiving woods for beginners. These woods are easy to cut, drill, rout, fasten, and finish. The wood is reasonably priced, is widely available, and produces attractive results. Once you've got a few softwood projects under your belt, you'll gain some insight about how to use your tools effectively and learn from those inevitable mistakes along the way. This sort of experience is invaluable, and it's a sensible way to prepare yourself for working with more challenging and expensive woods. Plus, you'll kick yourself less if you don't break your budget buying hardwood for your first project that simply doesn't work out as planned.

One way to spare your budget and still build an attractive, sturdy project is to use secondary woods like poplar and pine for those parts that don't show. On this drawer, the face is made of alder but the box is made of pine. When it's closed, no one will see the secondary wood.

How lumber is cut, seasoned & sized

Lumber mills use several methods for cutting logs into boards and drying the water-logged "green" wood into useable lumber. Once the lumber dries, it's trimmed and surfaced again to final dimensions, then carefully sorted and graded according to federally regulated standards before it's ready for shipment and sale. While you don't need a degree in forestry to be a woodworker, you'll buy more wisely if you have a general working knowledge of how boards are cut, seasoned, and sized.

From logs to boards: Logs are cut into boards in three ways, based on the species of tree as well as the quality and size of the logs. Sometimes a log will

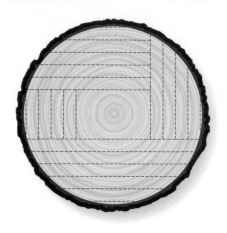

Plainsawn

End-grain

Plainsawn lumber is what you'll typically find at the lumberyard or home center. Look for a sweeping elliptical grain pattern on the face and concentric arches on the board ends.

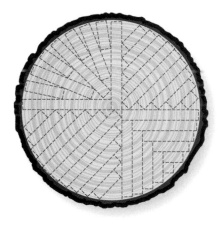

Quartersawn

End-grain

Depending on the species, quartersawn lumber will show straight grain or medullary rays and flecks on the face and end grain that is perpendicular or nearly so to the face.

be cut to take advantage of the lumber's attractive grain and figure, but more often it's cut to maximize yield. The typical cutting method used to mill what you'll find at the home center is called *plainsawing*. Here, the mill slices boards from a log until defects emerge, then the log is rotated one quarter-turn to saw from an adjacent face. Plainsawn lumber is easy to spot: the face grain shows a sweeping cathedral pattern of light and dark grain. The growth rings on the ends of boards resemble concentric arches stretching widthwise.

When picking through plainsawn lumber, choose boards with the flattest end-grain growth rings. These boards were cut closer to the perimeter of the tree, and they'll be less likely to cup when the humidity rises. Avoid boards with rings that radiate from a central point; these come from the center pith area of the log, and they'll be more prone to warping. Select board faces that show regular arches of light and dark grain rather than elliptical patterns. Boards with ellipsoid face grain may be hard to plane and will tend to bow.

Quartersawing is a second log-milling method. Here, the process involves splitting the log in half, then into four wedges. The wedges are ripped into boards so the growth rings are nearly perpendicular to the board faces. Quartersawn lumber will have tight, straight face grain rather than a cathedral grain pattern. Inspect the end grain and you'll see the growth rings look like straight, perpendicular lines. If the rings run at an angle to the face but aren't concentric or perpendicular, the board is actually riftsawn and not truly quartersawn.

When certain species such as oak and sycamore are quartersawn, the cut exposes striking translucent medullary rays and flecks that are highly prized and unmistakable. In other species such as Douglas fir, the growth rings will show through on the face grain as regular, parallel lines. Quartersawing produces fewer boards per log than plainsawing, and the process is time-consuming, so the lumber costs more. However, the lumber expands and contracts less than plainsawn boards, and the perpendicular growth ring orientation minimizes warpage. You'll rarely find quartersawn lumber at a general-purpose lumberyard or home center, but it's commonly sold through specialty lumberyards.

A third milling method, called *through-and-through* sawing (or *flat-sawing*), involves slicing through the log in successive passes without rotating it. Any defects present in the log end up in the boards because the log isn't turned to avoid them. This method maximizes the log's yield, but it produces a mixed bag of lumber cuts and qualities. Boards sawn through the center pith area will actually have a quartersawn region on either side of the pith.

If price were no object, most experts will argue that quartersawn lumber is the best value from the standpoint of durability and stability. However, since many wood types aren't available in quartersawn cuts, you'll have to settle for plainsawn or flatsawn lumber. Either of these cuts will make attractive, sturdy furniture if the lumber is properly dried first and if you take wood movement into account when designing your projects.

How lumber is dried: Once boards are cut from a log, they're considered "green" and unseasoned. At this stage, lumber contains a high percentage of water in its cells, sometimes exceeding the weight of the wood itself. Excess water must be removed and the lumber allowed to dry before the boards are suitable for woodworking purposes. Mills dry lumber to different percentages of moisture content, depending on how it will be sold and used.

The usual convention for drying lumber is to heat it for a few weeks in a kiln. Temperature, heat, and atmospheric pressure inside the kiln are precisely controlled and altered over time so the lumber dries evenly both inside and out. Drying times vary by species. Kiln-dried lumber will typically have a moisture content of about 6% to 10%. At this level, it's ideal for woodworking purposes. Framing lumber will have a moisture content around 19%, and treated lumber will be wetter still. This is one of the reasons why "2x" lumber is prone to warping: it still has more drying to do.

Some sawmills may air-dry lumber instead of baking it in a kiln. The drying process takes many months and even several years depending on relative humidity, but it's an economical alternative to investing in a kiln. With this drying method, strips of scrap wood called stickers are inserted between the boards in an orderly fashion when the lumber is first stacked to dry. Stickers act like spacers so air can circulate around each board. (Kiln-dried lumber also is separated by stickers for the same purpose.) Air-drying usually takes place outside with the stacks sheltered on top from direct sun and moisture. Sometimes the wood is stored in open-sided warehouses or simply covered with loose plastic. Over time, the boards are flipped and restacked to help accelerate drying.

Air-dried lumber typically won't reach the 6-10% moisture content of kiln-dried

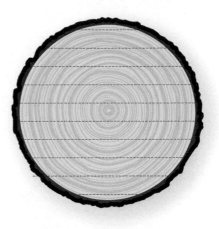

Flatsawn

End-grain

Flatsawn lumber may contain the center pith area of the tree, but boards also may resemble plain-sawn or quartersawn lumber, depending where on the log they are cut from. Sometimes, a board that contains the center pith of a large tree will actually have quartersawn areas on either side of the pith.

MOISTURE METERS

You can determine the moisture content of lumber before you use it, and sometimes even before you buy it, using a moisture meter. Moisture meters typically have a pair of sharpened probes that you press into a piece of lumber to take a reading, but some meters use internal sensors instead of probes. Better meters will also come with a calibration chart for setting the meter to test different wood species.

To take a reading, cut several inches off the end of a board, press the probes into the board and read the meter. It will indicate the percentage of moisture inside.

Meters are relatively reliable and easy to use, but they're expensive. Unless you buy lots of air-dried lumber, they probably aren't worth the cost. However, if you're buying roughsawn lumber from a specialty yard or directly from a sawmill, ask to have the wood moisture content measured in your presence. The yard should be willing to disclose this information to you readily. Or, they may have a moisture meter you can borrow to test the lumber yourself.

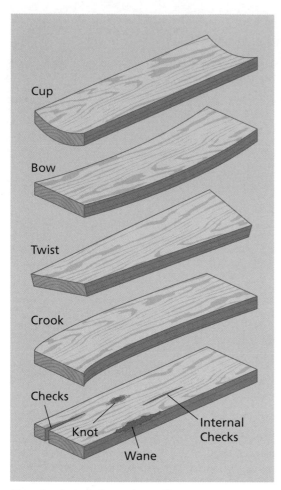

Cup

Bow

Twist

Crook

Checks

Knot

Wane

Internal
Checks

Four lumber defects that affect flatness include cup, bow, twist, and crook. Even boards that are flat along edges and faces may still contain other natural defects like knots, splits, checks, or waney edges.

It's easy to spot cup, bow, or twist in a piece of lumber by holding it near one end and sighting along its length.

lumber, but under careful drying conditions it will still make perfectly suitable woodworking lumber. In some instances, such as steam-bending, air-dried lumber is the preferred choice. Kiln drying collapses the wood cells, which makes the fibers less pliable than when they simply dry naturally. Some critics of air-drying argue that kiln-drying produces straighter lumber that expands and contracts less than air-dried boards. This claim is still debatable. From an economic standpoint, air-dried lumber is usually cheaper to buy than kiln-dried lumber.

Typical lumber defects

Lumber is hygroscopic, which means it absorbs and retains moisture like a sponge. Even after boards are dried, they'll still swell and shrink to some degree as the relative humidity of their surroundings changes. Boards "move" mostly across their width but also through their thickness to a lesser degree. They move very little lengthwise. Some amount of wood movement is unavoidable, and you'll need to account for it when you build your projects.

Lumber will expand or contract until the internal moisture content reaches equilibrium with the environment. Often, the process happens unevenly, which is part of the reason why lumber warps. Distortion is also a product of how the tree grew, what stresses were present inside the log, and how the boards were cut and dried. Lumber mills try to correct initial warping by planing lumber before they sell it, but that generally isn't the end of the story. Boards prone to warping will continue to do so at the lumberyard, in your shop and unfortunately even in your finished projects from time to time.

The four common types of distortion are bow, crook, cup, and twist (also called wind). You can easily check for these distortions by sighting down the face and edges of lumber. Bowing means the faces of a board curve lengthwise. A crooked board is flat across both faces but the edges curve. Cupping occurs when board faces curl but the edges are still flat. Boards with twist will have one or both ends curling so the faces aren't flat. Your eyes will detect even subtle deviations from flat surfaces. It's common to find several of these defects in a single board. Often, you'll be able to salvage boards with minor warping by cutting off the warped areas or splitting the board into flatter, smaller sections.

Aside from warp, lumber may have other natural defects that you'll need to deal with. Knots are common, but they're really only problematic if they're loose. Loose knots can get pulled free by a spinning bit or blade and become projectiles. Pockets of soft pitch and resin can foul blades, but they're mainly a problem when it comes to finishing. Paints and varnishes won't stick to soft wood pitch. Cut away pitch pockets to avoid problems. Sometimes you'll run across boards that have green, bluish, or grey discoloration or streaking called spalling. It's a sign of fungal growth. Once the board dries, the spalling process will stop, but the discoloration remains. Woodworkers often like to incorporate spalling into their work as a design element rather than remove it.

Checks are cracks that start at the ends of boards. Checking is a natural part of the drying process. They're easy to deal with by simply cutting away the defect a few inches in from the end of the crack. Sometimes you'll run across a board with cracks contained entirely inside the board, not starting from the end. It's best to avoid using these pieces. Inboard cracks can sometimes be attributed to a defect called case hardening, and they're the result of rapid, uneven kiln-drying. The cracks show where the board literally pulled itself apart trying to reach a moisture equilibrium with the atmosphere inside the kiln. The cracks you see on the surface are one thing, but there may be more hiding inside the board that you won't find until you machine it further. Be leery of a lumber supplier's kiln-drying practices if you find a case-hardened board—where there's one case-hardened board, there are bound to be more.

Some defects, like small, sound knots, are sometimes easy to cut off your lumber or even leave in place as design elements. Large, loose knots or deep splits are unacceptable. Remove these defects by cutting well clear of the problem areas.

Lumber sizing & grading: Walk the aisles of your home center or discount lumberyard and you'll find pine, cedar, and other softwood boards sold by "nominal" (or named) dimensions rather than actual dimensions. Hardwood boards sold to the general public are often milled nominally as well. Stretch a tape measure across these boards and you'll find that the nominal board size listed on the rack may say 1 × 4, but the thickness and width are actually ¾ inch by 3½ inches. The nominal dimensions indicate the size of the board when it was initially cut from the log, prior to drying, surfacing, and final trimming. Boards sized nominally up to 1 × 6 will be ¾ inch thick and ½ inch narrower than the named width. Boards wider than a nominal 6 inches will be ¾ inch narrower than their nominal width. In the nominal system of lumber sizing, the only actual dimension is length. You'll buy boards by the lineal foot, in lengths starting at 4 feet and going up to 10 or 12 ft. Nominal sizing is a bit confusing and not really helpful to the end user, but it doesn't take long to get used to the system.

Retail lumber outlets sometimes sell premium softwood and hardwood boards that aren't sized by quite the same nominal standards. The thickness will still be ¾ inch, but the width will match the actual dimension of the board. A 1 × 4 will be a full 4 inches wide. More common woods such as oak and pine won't be sold this way unless they are "select" cuts with no visual defects. Here's where you may also find a small sampling of less common lumber varieties including cherry, maple, walnut, or mahogany. Premium lumber is surfaced smooth on both faces and edges, and it may even be shrink-wrapped to help minimize warping. It will also be the most expensive lumber in the lumber area.

NOMINAL VS. FINISHED LUMBER SIZES

Nominal	Finished
1 × 2	¾ × 1½
1 × 3	¾ × 2½
1 × 4	¾ × 3½
1 × 6	¾ × 5½
1 × 8	¾ × 7¼
1 × 10	¾ × 9¼
1 × 12	¾ × 11¼
2 × 2	1½ × 1½
2 × 3	1½ × 2½
2 × 4	1½ × 3½
2 × 6	1½ × 5½
2 × 8	1½ × 7¼
2 × 10	1½ × 9¼
2 × 12	1½ × 11¼

QUARTERING SYSTEM FOR LUMBER THICKNESS (ROUGH DIMENSIONS)

Quartered size	Measured thickness
3/4	¾ inch
4/4	1 inch
5/4	1¼ inch
6/4	1½ inch
8/4	2 inch
10/4	2½ inch
12/4	3 inch

When you shop for hardwood lumber at a specialty yard, you won't find it sized nominally. Lumber thickness is sized according to a quartering system. Boards that are 1 inch thick are sized as 4/4, called "four quarter," and it means the thickness is equal to four quarter inches. Generally, 4/4 is the thinnest cut, and thicknesses go up from there. Five, six, eight, ten, and even twelve-quarter thicknesses are common for many hardwoods. These sizes translate into 1¼, 1½, 2, 2½ and 3 inch rough thicknesses.

Specialty hardwoods are sold in random widths and lengths rather than standardized dimensions. Since the sizing varies, you buy this lumber by volume, not by length and width. The unit of measurement is the "board foot," which equals a board unit measuring 1 inch thick, 12 inches wide and 12 inches long—a volume of 144 cubic inches. Of course each board will have different dimensions, so the proportions you'll get per board foot will vary. Every specialty hardwood board you buy will be priced according to board feet, regardless of thickness, width, or length.

The easiest way to calculate the price of a board is to measure thickness, width, and length in inches, multiply these numbers together, then divide the total by 144 to determine the number of board feet. The lumberyard will post a board foot price for every quartered thickness of each species. Multiply your number of board feet by the board foot price to arrive at the board's overall price, not including applicable sales tax.

Both softwoods and hardwoods are graded according to federal standards to assure consistent quality within the lumber commodities industry. Softwoods are categorized with various grade names that include B Select and Better, C Select, D Select, Superior Finish, Prime Finish, No. 1 Common and No. 2 Common. The grade is often stamped right on the board or specified on a label stapled to the end. These grades indicate how many natural blemishes a board may have, as well as the size of the defects. From highest to lowest grade, B Select is the clearest grade and No. 2 Common will have the most blemishes. You'll rarely be able to pick and choose from among these grades if you shop at retail lumber outlets. They'll likely stock a select grade and a common grade only.

Hardwoods are graded by different standards than softwoods. Boards are evaluated in terms of the percentage of defect-free lumber they contain. From highest to lowest percentages of clear lumber, the grades include Firsts and Seconds, Select, and numbers 1, 2A, 2B, 3A, and 3B Common. Lumber graded as Firsts and Seconds (FAS) or Select must be 83⅓% clear, while No. 3B Common need only be 25% clear. Not even specialty yards will stock all these grades, but you'll find FAS or Select and at least one common grade of each species sold there.

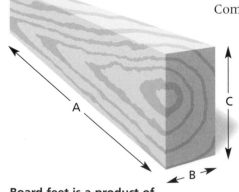

Board feet is a product of multiplying the length (A) times the width (C) times the thickness (B). When each of these measurements are made in inches, divide the answer by 144 to determine the number of board feet.

Surfacing options: Softwood lumber is usually planed smooth on all surfaces when you buy it. So is the hardwood you'll find at discount lumberyards and home centers. If you buy lumber directly from the sawmill or a specialty yard, all the final surfacing might not be done. This is particularly true for hardwoods. What you'll find instead may be lumber with no finished surfaces, called "roughsawn;" boards with two surfaced faces but rough edges, called "Surfaced Two Sides" or "S2S;" and lumber with the edges and faces planed smooth, called "Surfaced Four Sides," or "S4S." The more surfacing the mill does for you, the higher the board foot cost will be. If you have access to a surface planer and jointer, roughsawn lumber offers great value, but you won't know how the finished lumber will look until you remove the rough surfaces. Some yards will allow you to take a few shavings off roughsawn lumber with a hand plane to help evaluate the underlying grain pattern or figure. Ask before you try this. For yards that don't allow a sneak peak, you'll have to take your chances on what you get.

Three common surfacing options are shown here. The board on top is "S4S," which means both faces and edges are planed flat. The middle board is "S2S," with only the faces planed and not the edges. The bottom board is simply roughsawn with no additional planing. Generally, the more surfacing that's done for you, the more it will cost at the yard.

Sources for buying lumber

Your local home center or lumberyard will be a convenient source for lumber, but there are other options as well. Here are a few to consider:

Sawmills: If you live in a wooded state, there's bound to be a sawmill somewhere near those forests, and many of these smaller businesses gladly sell lumber to the general public. Check your local Yellow Pages under sawmills for possible sources. You'll probably pay less money buying locally, and you'll have the satisfaction of knowing you are using lumber from locally grown trees. Be aware that these sawmills probably won't kiln-dry their lumber, so you'll need to check it for moisture content and possibly store it for some time before it's usable. You may also need to do all the surface planing and jointing work yourself—the wood likely will be roughsawn if it comes from a small mill. Some adventurous woodworkers even buy portable, trailer-mounted sawmills and saw their own lumber from trees they fell themselves.

Specialty lumberyards: Some lumberyards specialize in furniture lumber, usually hardwoods of many sorts. If you need an unusual size or species for your project, these are the places to call. Large specialty yards buy roughsawn stock in volume and either sell it this way or do some degree of surfacing. Some yards sell to the general public, so you can buy any quantity of lumber down to a single board. Other yards target their business to cabinet shops and professional woodworkers, so there may be a minimum board foot requirement for purchasing there. In these cases, talk with other woodworkers you know and pool your resources to buy larger quantities of lumber together, then split the cost.

Woodworking stores: There are several national chains of woodworking stores with outlets in most large cities. These stores carry a variety of hardwood lumber species including many hard-to-find exotics. You'll also find reference books,

When buying graded hardwood, keep in mind that FAS grade isn't qualitatively better lumber than lower grades, it just has fewer natural defects. Cherry lumber is cherry lumber, whether it's FAS or No. 2 Common. The issue here is how many defects are acceptable to you. For rustic projects, maybe a few knots here and there will add character, and you can save money buying lower-grade stock. If you're building a project with smaller parts, lumber with more defects may work just fine. Once the defects are cut away, there may be ample clear wood to make the parts you need.

tools and unique hardware. The sales staff can provide helpful advice about what wood might work best for your project. Generally, the lumber you'll find at these stores will be premium grade FAS, and though there may be many species to choose from, the prices tend to be higher than buying from larger lumberyards.

Catalogs/mail-order sources: Large lumber suppliers often run ads in woodworking magazines and offer catalogs of their lumber inventories. Most now have web sites. If you're looking for an unusual species or cut, or if you plan to order lumber in volume, mail-order sources can offer good value. Reputable lumber companies will offer satisfaction guarantees on what you buy since generally you'll be buying lumber sight-unseen. Ask about return policies in case you receive defective or unsatisfactory wood. Be sure to inquire about moisture content and lumber grade as well. You should know the specific sizes of lumber you need and be prepared to make alterations if the lumber supplier doesn't offer the dimensions you're after. Don't forget to ask about shipping costs—you're paying for it.

On-line auctions: In our Internet-driven world, you have the option to bid on lumber using on-line auction houses such as eBay. Internet lumber sources are all over the board. You may be bidding on lumber from small mills, lumberyards, or even the results of a fallen backyard tree. Anyone can sell lumber this way, not just reputable dealers. However, most sellers auctioning their lumber do this sort of thing regularly.

Lumber quality will be difficult to evaluate, and you'll take more risks buying by "virtual" auction than from a dedicated mail-order source or a store or yard close to you. Before bidding, e-mail or call the seller and ask the same questions you'd direct to a mail-order lumberyard. Inquire about moisture content, lumber grade, and any guarantee that may apply to your purchase. Remember also that shipping isn't included in the final winning bid—that's extra. Ask the seller to estimate your shipping costs as well as any other charges that may apply, such as crating or wrapping your wood. Most sellers will be happy to disclose the details, because it reduces their risk of buyers failing to pay once the auction ends. Lumber auctions pose the same benefits and risks to you as any other Internet auction. You may snatch the wood for a song, or it may end up costing you as much as buying it retail. Don't bid more than you are willing to pay, and protect yourself against unexpected surprises by asking lots of questions before becoming the winning bidder.

Storing lumber

Dry lumber isn't difficult to store, provided you keep it in a dry place with a reasonable amount of fresh air exchange. If your shop is in the basement, run a dehumidifier during summer months. For particularly damp basements, you may want to wrap dry lumber in 4- or 6-mil polyethylene to protect it from the surrounding damp air.

It's tough to control humidity levels in garage, shed, and other outbuilding shops, particularly if the shop doubles as a place to park cars and the garage door gets opened and closed every day. One preventive measure you can take is to separate the boards in a stack with stickers to improve air circulation. Keep lumber off of dirt or concrete floors to prevent moisture from wicking up and saturating the wood. If your garage shop has a large accessible attic, store your lumber there. The air will be drier and warmer than near the floor.

You might buy air-dried lumber that's only partially seasoned. When there's more drying to do, store the lumber outside on a hard, flat surface with stickers in between. The goal here is to get as much air circulating around the boards as possible so they dry evenly and relatively quickly. Keep the bottom board off the ground with stickers, too. Put a cover over the top of the stack, but keep the sides open to promote air movement. A plastic tarp weighed down with cinder blocks makes a good top cover. Or use a piece of corrugated metal. If you have a carport or other open-sided building that offers shelter from the elements, stack your lumber there to dry and forego the top cover.

As soon as the moisture content drops below 14%, move boards inside where they are safe from the elements. The amount of time it takes to reach this level will depend on factors like the relative humidity in your area and the species of wood you are drying. Some will say that you should plan on drying lumber one year for every inch of board thickness, but this is just a general guideline. A better way to track the drying process is to check it periodically with a moisture meter.

Once in the shop, the best way to store long lumber is horizontally on shelves or in a stack elevated off the floor on blocks. If you store boards vertically, they can warp. Make sure your shelving is solidly built and supports the lumber every 16 inches or so lengthwise. This will also help prevent warping. Lumber shorter than four feet can be stored either horizontally or vertically, whichever is more convenient.

Allow new lumber to acclimate to your shop air for a few weeks before using it. This may seem like a long time to wait, but it gives the wood a chance to distort some as it reaches a level of moisture equilibrium with the air in your shop.

Sheet goods overview

Manufactured sheet goods are an economical alternative to board lumber for creating wide panels. Plywood, particleboard, and other sheet materials tend to stay flatter than solid wood, although they aren't impervious to some warping and swelling as the humidity rises. Home centers, lumberyards and specialized sheet good

If you store lumber in the basement, run a dehumidifier during humid summer months and check the relative humidity near the lumber with a hygrometer. Separating boards in a stack with scraps of lumber called stickers is also a good practice. Stickers promote air circulation around each board.

companies offer many useful products for your projects. Here's a brief overview of what you may find:

Plywood: Plywood is generally sold in 4 foot × 8 foot sheets in thicknesses ranging from ¼ inch up to ¾ inch. Your supplier may sell half or quarter sheets as well. The core material is usually multiple thin layers of wood veneer sandwiched together so the grain pattern alternates from ply to ply. The alternating veneers give plywood its strength and dimensional stability. Plywood cores are also made of various grades of ground wood pulp or strips of solid wood. The plys may have voids here and there, depending on the grade of material.

Your local source for building materials will probably stock two families of plywood: construction plywood and higher-grade plywood suitable for cabinetry and general woodworking. Plywood made for construction purposes has rough layers of veneer on the surfaces made of various softwoods. The outer face veneer is graded alphabetically by quality. "B-C" plywood is a common sheet material used for sheathing and subfloors. The "B" face will have fewer imperfections than the "C" face, but both will have some irregularities. Reserve this kind of construction plywood for utility projects only. Treated plywood is another construction-grade sheet material suitable for exterior uses.

Better grades of plywood for woodworking, cabinetry, and the like are easy to spot: Look for smooth birch, oak, or maple face veneers on the sheets. One face of the veneer is rated A through D from highest to lowest quality, and the other face has a numeric rating from 1 through 4. Hardwood plywood will be much more expensive than construction-grade plywood, which should come as no surprise. The outer veneer is furniture quality and requires little sanding. If you need plywood with a face veneer that matches other solid wood in your project, you can order it covered with virtually any species of wood veneer, including cherry, walnut, mahogany, pine, quartersawn or riftsawn lumbers, and even exotics.

Cabinet-grade plywoods come in a wide variety of surface veneer options. Your local home center probably stocks oak and birch, but you can special-order walnut, pine, cherry, mahogany, maple, and other veneers as well.

Another high-grade plywood product worth noting is Baltic birch. Made in northern Europe, Baltic birch is relatively easy to find in the U.S., particularly from lumberyards that stock specialty plywoods. Baltic birch has about twice the number of veneer layers as cabinet-grade plywood sheets, and there are no voids between the layers. The sheets are sized metrically with the overall proportions of a sheet being smaller than standard plywood. A full sheet is approximately 5 feet × 5 feet. Baltic birch is an ideal choice for drawer parts, cabinetry, or shop jigs and fixtures.

Melamine & particleboard: Particleboard is the sheet material that looks like ground-up wood glued together. Melamine is a general term for particleboard covered with a colored facing of resin-impregnated paper. The coating creates a durable surface that's easy to keep clean. White melamine is most common, but you can also buy it in black, beige, or gray. It's sold in full 4 × 8 sheets and in narrower shelving with a bullnosed edge.

Both melamine and particleboard are made of coarsely ground wood pulp and adhesive resins pressed together under extreme heat and pressure. They're less expensive than plywood and somewhat more dimensionally stable, provided the sheets stay dry. Melamine and particleboard will swell and crumble in the presence of moisture. Melamine is a good fuss-free choice for box and cabinet interiors because you won't need to paint or finish it. Particleboard can be painted, but usually its rough surface texture shows through the paint. Use particleboard for shop fixtures, jigs, shelving, and other utility projects. Melamine and particleboard machine easily, but they don't hold nails, screws, or other fasteners as well as plywood. Cut or routed edges will be rough and filled with tiny voids.

Medium-density fiberboard: Commonly known by its acronym, MDF, medium-density fiberboard is essentially particleboard made with finely ground wood fibers. MDF is commonly sold in ½- and ¾-inch thicknesses, but other thicknesses are available by special order. It costs about the same as particleboard and less than melamine. You may even find MDO (medium-density overlay), which has a water-resistant paper coating on one face and an MDF core.

Other sheet good options include hardboard (top), medium-density fiberboard (center) and medium-density overlay (bottom). All three are good options for painted panels, drawer bottoms, or shop jigs.

The material consistency of MDF is much finer than particleboard. In fact, MDF hardly looks like wood at all. As a general-purpose building material, MDF is hard to beat. The fibers are pressed together under such extreme pressure that MDF machines and sands without voids or tearout. It holds fasteners reasonably well and is an excellent choice for painted projects. However, the machining process creates copious amounts of fine dust. Be sure to wear a respirator and keep the windows open when machining or sanding MDF.

Another disadvantage to this otherwise useful and versatile sheet material is weight. The density of MDF makes it extremely heavy. A single ¾-inch-thick sheet weighs nearly 100 pounds—about twice the heft of a sheet of ¾-inch plywood. If you need the smoothness offered by MDF but the part you're making isn't a critical structural member, use ½-inch material instead.

Hardboard: Hardboard, also known by the brand name Masonite, is essentially a darker, denser form of MDF with the same general characteristics. It is sold as full 4 foot × 8 foot sheets as well as smaller half and quarter sheets. This material is much thinner than MDF; you'll find it in ⅛-inch and ¼-inch thicknesses. Hardboard is an economical material for building drawer bottoms and the back panels of cabinets or painted bookcases. It makes durable, reusable patterns for template routing (see page 82) or as parts for other workshop jigs and fixtures.

Chapter 3
PROJECT PLANNING

The first step of any woodworking project involves planning. Simple projects may take just a bit of forethought before you're ready to build, but more complicated furniture usually takes much more noodling. Either way, some degree of planning is essential. Try to think of the "shop phase" of woodworking as an exercise in delayed gratification, preceded by time at the drawing board. If you're poised in front of a stack of lumber with saw in hand and no paper plans on the bench, good luck! Chances are, your best intentions will be met with some degree of frustration when you miscut a table leg, build a drawer that won't fit its opening, or realize at a late hour that you are two boards short.

Project planning has three basic stages: determining what you want to build, working out the details through drawings and prototypes, then calculating material and cutting lists from your drawings. This chapter will introduce you to each stage so you can plan your next project confidently and have a good time building it. After all, woodworking should be enjoyable, right? Planning first will keep you smiling later.

Deciding what to build

The motivation to build something has any number of sources. Maybe your family has outgrown the kitchen table and you want to replace it with something a bit out of the ordinary. You can design any table you want and customize it to suit your individual needs or tastes. Maybe you've had your eye on an Arts & Crafts sideboard at the local furniture gallery, but it's priced beyond your means. Building one yourself allows you, rather than the furniture retailer, to control the quality and cost. Possibly you just want to try some new woodworking techniques or tools to expand your skill base.

Gathering ideas: Whatever your motivation may be for building something, chances are you've already thought about it enough to have some initial ideas about a design. The idea-gathering stage is important. It's the time to let your imagination go without com-

Keep a file folder of clippings for those furniture styles and designs that appeal to you. Someday they may serve as the inspiration for a project you build.

mitting to any one notion. Feed your ideas with lots of concrete options so you can start to clarify a design. Furniture stores are good places to examine a variety of furniture styles up close. Pay attention to the furnishings you find in your friends' homes, as well as what's for sale through furniture catalogs. Leaf through woodworking magazines and project books. You'll find loads of published plans for every conceivable woodworking project in an assortment of styles. Hit some web sites of professional woodworkers to see galleries of their work, and download and print out examples that look interesting. Keep catalog or magazine clippings, advertisements, photocopies, and photographs of possible projects in a file folder so you can refer to them often.

In your ongoing search for ideas, you'll discover that furniture follows some classic style trends, and it always has. Certainly everything you make doesn't have to conform to an accepted style, but basic furniture design is the end result of centuries of trial and error. Study proportions of cabinetry, tables, chairs, and chests to get a sense for how furniture functions in harmony with the human body. You'll know a comfortable chair when you sit in one, even if you can't pinpoint why it feels so supportive. Seat size, leg height, and the tilt of the back rest are all factors that contribute to comfort. (Seat height and depth are around 15 to 18 inches; the seat width is a bit wider still. Arm leans are generally about 8 to 10 inches above the seat.) These proportions have been tested over time. Bookcases are generally not taller than you can reach, so books remain accessible without using a step stool. (They usually have a maximum height of 76 inches.) Drawers are deep enough to store a layer of items, but not deep enough to lose them. (Keep general-purpose drawers shallower than 6 inches.) Dining tables tend to be wide enough to accommodate place settings on either side as well as a few serving dishes. However, they shouldn't be so wide as to make it impossible to reach across easily. (Each place setting around a table should be about 24 to 30 inches wide.)

Evaluate your skills, budget, and tools: Keep your skill level in mind as you study furniture. Furniture with relief carvings, delicate inlays, or parts that join at angles or curves will be more difficult to build than pieces with straight lines and minimal ornamentation. If you're just starting out, consider making projects in the Arts & Crafts, Shaker, and country styles. These are good options for building sturdy furniture without needing advanced woodworking skills or a full arsenal of machinery. Try a new technique here or there within the furniture style that suits your skill level to keep every project interesting. Your roster of skills will grow bit by bit without jeopardizing the success of a whole project.

Building sensibly means working with some project budget in mind. When your pockets for a project aren't deep, the dollars will go farther by building with ¾-inch lumber rather than thick slabs of exotic hardwood. It's almost always true that the larger your project becomes physically, the more it costs. One way to help keep from blowing the budget on big projects is to substitute sheet goods for solid lumber. Sheet goods are generally less expensive, and you can steer clear of the wood movement issues you'll face when designing panels made of solid wood. Remember to include the cost of special hardware your project will need, such as slides, hinges, doorknobs, and drawer pulls. These items definitely add to the bottom line of what your project costs to build. So do those "extras" such as a new router bit, a package of sandpaper, or the cans of varnish and stain you'll need for finishing.

Before embarking on a project, have a look around your workshop at the tools you own. Do you have all the equipment you'll need for cutting out your project parts, shaping the edges, assembling wood panels, or smoothing the part surfaces? If your project parts are small and curved, how will you safely cut the tiny curves? A scroll saw is the best tool for this task. Will you need one, or can you modify the design or accomplish the task another way? Think through the construction phase of the project and how you'll manage each machining step. Otherwise, you could end up midway through a project and stumped over how to proceed. If you can't accomplish the project without buying a new tool, will your budget support the expenditure?

Building from published plans or from scratch: Designing from scratch is a wonderful way to take full ownership of a project, but it's not always the wisest move for beginners. You'll need to evaluate whether the greater good is to make something totally new and unique or follow the plans of someone else. Your inspired design may work beautifully, but you're taking on the full brunt of determining size, shape, joinery, materials, and tooling methods for executing your idea. Published plans aren't always accurate (often they aren't!), but they're darn close. Accomplished magazine and book editors or seasoned woodworkers have worked out the design bugs for you in advance. You'll have the benefit of measured drawings, a material list, some helpful how-to photos, and a finished example of the project.

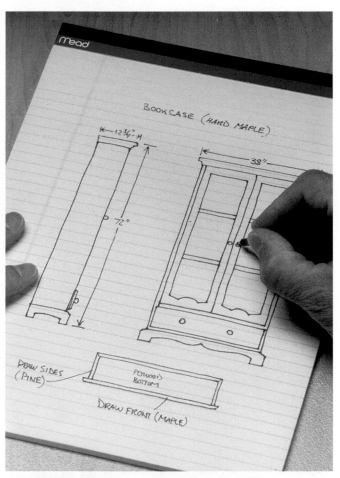

From ideas to sketches

To help firm up your project ideas and make them tangible, they need to be drawn out on paper. Drawings lay all the groundwork of your design and help you avoid pitfalls. Don't let the paper stage intimidate you. Starting is as easy as making crude sketches to give your ideas some grit.

Concept sketches: The first round of drawings, called concept sketches, should be almost as free-flowing as your ideas for a project. At this stage, you are still playing around with any number of possibilities. Try to doodle and sketch several different options for what you want to build, incorporating as many different features as you like. If it's a chest of drawers, make a half dozen equal-sized rectangles to serve as the overall chest shape, and try a different drawer arrangement on each rectangle. If none of your drawer configurations will

Collect your thoughts about a new project idea and try some design elements on for size by making a concept sketch. Make it freehand and without restrictions to see how your ideas gel.

work, make the rectangle taller or shorter, or try turning it on its side, then play around with the drawer options again.

Sketch a couple views of your project while you're at it. You'll probably start with a front view, but draw a side view as well. A top view is helpful for objects like chairs that have more parts relating to one another than, for example, a table with a square top. Plot some rough dimensions for height, width, and depth on your drawings, and do the best you can to make thicker or thinner parts look that way on the sketch. There's really no need to draft these sketches with perfectly straight lines or exacting details. That happens later. Use lots of inexpensive paper and don't be afraid to erase or start over. When you happen on a feature you like in your sketch, trace it onto your next sketch so you can save time redrawing it. You might find it helpful to grab the colored pencils and shade a sketch in.

Once you've got an overall form sketched out, think about the kinds of joinery you'll use to assemble the project, as well as other features that need closer attention. Will you build the drawers with rabbet joints or dovetails? How will the doors swing or a drawer slide open and closed? What sort of edge shape would look attractive around a tabletop? Will the legs of your chair design have a graceful curve or a gradual taper on two sides? Now is a good time to think about these kinds of details. Make some additional freehand sketches to figure these issues out. Detail drawings of this sort help you simplify the complicated aspects of your project. Make these sketches as large as you need to get a realistic perspective on proportions.

The concept stage is an excellent time to think about some practical issues as well. First off, be mindful of both form and function. Will the style of your

Among the many design issues you'll face in each project is what hardware to choose for the project. Knobs, pulls and handles add character and "curb appeal" to the project, while hinges, slides and other mechanical components affect function.

project blend in with other furniture in the room? If it's somewhat different than the rest, consider adding a few design details to bring it closer to the style of furniture it will live with, or build it from the same wood. Will the project fit the space you have in mind for it? Is there enough room for doors and drawers to open without blocking windows, doorways, or heat registers? Can you build the project in your shop and get it out the door or lift it without a crane once it's finished?

There are also hardware and other lumber decisions to make. What hardware will you use for the project? The outer hardware can add distinctive flair, while hinges, catches, and slides impact how the wood parts fit together and move. This is particularly true for drawers and doors. Hardware need not limit your creativity, but it will impact how closely you can build what you sketch. Think also about the lumber you'll need to buy for building your project. If, for instance, you are designing a table with 3-inch-square legs, how will you make the legs? Can you find solid wood in this size or will you have to glue individual boards together?

Making prototypes: Prototypes are essentially rough models of what you plan to build. Whether built to a small scale or full size, they provide a three-dimensional representation of your project. Make scale models with whatever odds and ends you have on hand. Scrap-bin wood, cardboard, or foam-core board all make good building materials to assemble into miniatures. Make the model a convenient size, maybe the same size as your sketches, to keep all the proportions consistent. Join the parts with tape, hot-melt glue, staples, or whatever is quick and easy. The point is to enhance your sketches, not create elaborate doll-sized furniture.

One way to bring your concept sketches to life in three dimensions is to create a miniature prototype.

A full-sized prototype need not be carefully detailed to provide the information you need, so keep it simple. Here, a prototype that helps you determine, say, the size of the table top and overall height may be all you need it to do. Place the prototype in your dining room. How does the size of the table work in the space? Will all your dining room chairs fit around it?

If you're building a chair, full-size prototyping is essential. A sketch won't tell you a thing about how a piece of furniture fits your body. Use scrap lumber and plywood connected with drywall screws to construct your prototype chair. Now sit on the prototype. How does it feel? Probably not great to start with. If not, start tweaking the prototype. Add more scraps to raise the seat height. Tilt the back a little more or less, and move armrests up or down to improve the ergonomic aspects of the chair. Work at the prototype until you find a pleasing fit, then keep the model to measure off those important dimensions when you make your measured scale drawings.

Full-size prototypes will clearly indicate whether the proportions and features you have in mind will fit the human body or a physical space properly. A little time spent prototyping before you build can save you lots of money and frustration later.

Drafting scale drawings

When you're happy with your sketches and prototypes, it's time to draw the project accurately. It isn't difficult to make construction drawings that provide a reliable representation of what your finished project will look like. Line drawings of this sort are usually drawn to a smaller scale than the actual project, and all the dimensions are true to that scale. Two-dimensional drawings, called *orthographics*, come first. Here's where you'll draft the elevation drawings, which include the front, side, and back views. Top and bottom views, called plan drawings, can also be helpful. Detail drawings round out the orthographic package. The measurements you determine in your plan and elevation drawings can then be used to create a three-dimensional drawing, called an *isometric*. When done carefully, you can use your collection of scale drawings to create accurate lists for buying lumber and cutting parts.

It's helpful to fit several views of your project onto each page of your drawings. The more information you can see at a glance, the easier it will be to keep the overall project in mind. More importantly, you can extend measurements from one drawing up or over on the page to help draw another view. The scale won't change between the elevation and plan views, so common measurements are transferable. Try to have the front,

DRAFTING SUPPLIES YOU'LL NEED

An art supply store will stock all the drafting tools necessary to make scale drawings. Buy the following items and you'll have everything you'll need to get started:
- Mechanical pencil with fine, hard leads
- Soft gum eraser
- Architect's scale or ruler
- 45° × 45° drafting triangle
- 30° × 60° drafting triangle
- T-square
- Drawing board (around 2 feet × 3 feet) or portable drafting table with a sliding rule
- Vellum, graph or other translucent drawing paper
- 4- and 8-inch compasses
- French curve

ARCHITECT'S SCALE

To make reduced-scale drawings, you'll need an architect's scale. Essentially, it's a three-sided ruler with 11 different scales. Architects use these scales to measure foot increments, but the scales work just as well for sizing down inches. Five of the six edges of the ruler are divided into two scales, one scale reading left to right and the other from right to left. Each scale plots a different fraction of an inch to represent whole foot or inch units. For instance, one edge has both a ¾ and ⅜ scale. The ¾ scale, reading left to right, plots fourteen ¾-inch units plus a 15th unit subdivided into twelve parts. With this scale, you could draft a woodworking drawing where each ¾-inch unit equals 1 full inch or 1 full foot. The ⅜ scale includes 28 units measuring ⅜ inch, and these read right to left. One edge of the ruler, labeled "16," is a full-size inch scale divided into 1/16-inch increments. The "3" and "1½" scales plot units larger than 1 inch. These are handy to enlarge small details.

Once you've chosen a scale for your drawings, an architect's scale isn't difficult to use. Plot line lengths on your drawing using whole units on the scale, starting from the "0" mark. Then add any fractions of a foot or inch using the subdivided end unit of the scale. The only real trick is to keep from inadvertently flipping the ruler and measuring off the wrong scale.

side, and top views on one page.

The first task is to choose a scale for your drawings. Larger scales make it easier to draw fine details, but the size of your project and paper will influence how big a scale you can use. To pick the scale, find the largest dimension of your project and measure this distance on your paper using several different edges of the architect's scale. Pick the largest scale that affords you enough extra space to draw a couple other views. For example, if your project's largest dimension is 4 feet, the ¾ scale will make this line 3 inches long. Since the other measurements of the project are shorter than 3 inches, you should be able to draw several plan and elevation views on two sheets of standard-sized paper taped together. With this scale, your proportion would be ¾ inch equals 1 foot, or ¾" = 1'.

The usual convention for laying out elevation and plan drawings is to start with the front view roughly centered top to bottom on the paper and near the left edge. Top and bottom views are drawn directly above and below the front view. Side and back views are drawn to the right of the front view and in line with it. This way, all the relevant widths of the top and bottom views can be taken directly from the front view by drawing vertical guide lines up and down from it. The project's overall height and other vertical measurements can be transferred to the side and back views with guide lines drawn horizontally off the front view.

Draw the front view first, using your architect's scale for plotting distances and the T-square and triangles for making horizontal, perpendicular, and angular lines. Add elements from your concept sketches, such as leg shapes and the

Eventually your concept sketches and prototyping should culminate in making a set of scaled plan and elevation drawings. Careful measurements and accurate line drawings are essential here.

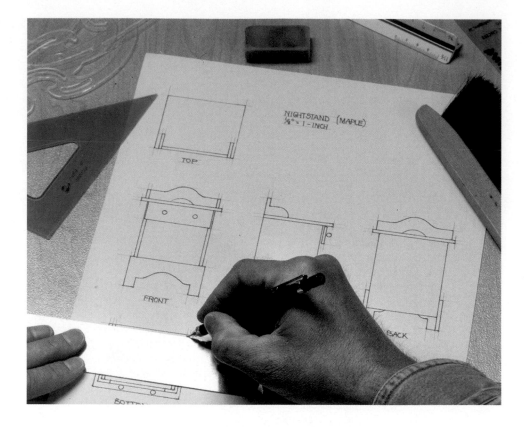

locations of knobs, pulls, or hinges. If your prototypes provided helpful information about proportions, be sure to include those dimensions here. These drawings should tell the whole story about your design, so take the time to make each view information-packed. Once the front view is complete, extend faint lines up and down from the front view to plot the overall width of the top and bottom views. Use the architect's scale to determine the depth of these plan views, then fill in the necessary details. Draw the side and back views next. Use the T-square to project as many common lines over from the front view as possible to mark part heights on the side and back views.

You'll need to determine what sorts of detail drawings to make for your project. Joints are good candidates for detail drawings because they allow you to work out the best proportions for the parts. Consider making detail drawings for joints that attach legs to aprons or stretchers, door stiles and rails, drawer box corners, and so forth. It's also helpful to draw details showing how doors and hinges relate, and how to size a drawer to leave clearance for metal drawer slides. Any aspects of the project that are difficult to see in your plan and elevation views or are difficult to work through in your mind should get mapped out in detail drawings. If you need to determine how some aspect of your project will look on the inside, make a drawing showing part of the project cut away in cross-section to help clarify things. Imagine slicing a line down the center of your project or project part. Draw what you'd find if you were to do this.

Draw the details or cross-sections right on the same pages as the plan and elevation drawings, if they'll fit. This way you'll keep the details close to the overall drawings of the project, so related information stays together. Draw the details at a larger scale than the rest of your drawings or even full size.

Once all your drawings are finished, you should feel confident about your design as well as how you'll build it. If some aspects still seem vague, you probably aren't finished drawing the necessary details.

After you've drawn the plan and elevation views, add leader lines alongside the drawings to show the necessary measurements. The drawings should include measurements for overall height, width, and depth. Make these stand alone so they are easy to find. Then draw more leader lines in from the overall dimension lines and divvy them up to show particular part dimensions. All the smaller dimensions you plot on these inner leader lines should add up to the overall dimensions. You'll develop a cutting list to accompany your drawings, which can provide dimensions that won't fit on the other drawings.

Full-sized detail drawings of joint parts help to ensure that you'll cut parts accurately the first time. The more intricate the joint, the more beneficial the detail drawing will be.

Creating an isometric drawing: Use the measurements created in the 2D plan and elevation drawings to make a three-dimensional representation of the project. There are a couple options here, but the easiest 3D drawing to make is called an *isometric*. Basically, an isometric drawing renders the project from a front corner so you can see the front, one side and the top from an angle. Usually, the vantage point is the front left corner. Isometrics are created primarily with vertical and 30° lines, drawn with the 30° × 60° triangle and the T-square. What's convenient about isometric drawings is that each line is at the same scale as the plan and elevation drawings. You'll take the measurements directly off those drawings and apply them to the isometric. Although the drawing will be dimensionally correct and to scale, it creates a skewed perception of depth because the project doesn't get smaller as its depth increases. The background is as large as the foreground. However, even with the distortion, isometrics are easier to draw than perspective views, which show a more true representation of depth.

Let's use the typical left corner vantage point to draw an isometric. The actual left corner line is the left line of your front view drawing, drawn vertically and to the same length. Now draw the bottom edge of the project front by scribing a line at 30° up and to the right of the left corner line. Make the bottom edge of the project's left side by drawing a 30° line up and to the left of the front corner line.

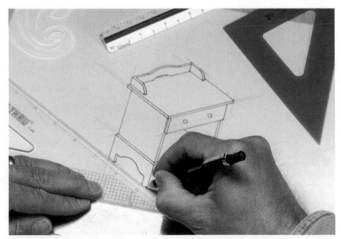

Isometric drawings, which are essentially combinations of vertical and 30° lines, transform your 2D drawings into three-dimensional forms.

Extend height lines up from the ends of these angled lines to create the project's overall height. Draw four more 30° lines left and right to form the top of the project and, essentially, the box that will contain the full project. From here, use the measurements in your plan and elevation drawings to fill in the details inside the

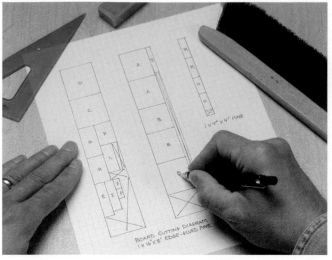

Cutting diagrams make it easier to determine how much board lumber and sheet goods you need to buy. Draw common board sizes to scale, then lay out and label every part.

isometric box and "flesh out" the project. When parts are inset from the outer faces of the isometric box, use faint 30° or vertical lines drawn in from the box faces to determine where to position these parts.

Drawing curves, circles, and parts with non-square angles requires more careful description than we'll explain here. These curved lines will appear skewed on the sides of an isometric drawing to mimic the way they look on the side of any object seen in three dimensions.

Another method of drawing an object in three dimensions is called *perspective*. This technique provides a more realistic impression of depth than an isometric view, but it's not as easy to draw. The measurements for "depth" lines cannot be taken directly off your plan and elevation drawings like they can for isometrics. Instead, the illusion of depth is created by using two vanishing points. These points, drawn on a horizontal line near the top of the drawing, represent two points on the horizon, behind the drawing. One vantage point is located near the right edge of the paper and the other is near the left edge. While the vertical lines of a perspective drawing are all drawn at 90° to the bottom edge of the paper, the horizontal lines of the drawing extend from the vertical lines to the vantage points. This technique makes the project appear progressively smaller from front to back, just like objects really do when we look at them at an angle from front to back.

Developing shopping & cutting lists

Once your plan, elevation, and detail drawings are complete, use them to create a shopping list that tallies up the lumber you'll need to buy and another list of every part in the project with its exact dimensions spelled out.

Itemizing a shopping list involves calculating the amount of lumber and sheet material that will be required for your project. The easiest way to do this is to make scale drawings of boards in their common lumberyard sizes to represent a virtual stack of lumber. If your project includes sheet goods, draw full and half sheets as well. Then draw each part of your project on these board and sheet good models to map out a rough idea of how much material will be required. These become cutting diagrams. Try to sketch the parts with reasonable accuracy and to scale, or at least parcel each board into squares or rectangles that represent the overall size of the parts. Label each part with a number, letter, or name to account for it on your cutting diagrams. Work carefully to be sure every part finds a place on a cutting diagram. If you need more than one type or thickness of lumber, label the cutting diagrams to keep these particulars clear.

Cutting diagrams have their limitations. For one, they can't account for the natural defects you'll encounter on the boards you buy. Rarely will you be able to maximize every inch of the board you draft as a cutting diagram. Remember also that you'll lose a certain amount of material to the saw blade just cutting the parts out of a board. Sometimes you'll create a shopping list from cutting diagrams and find that the lumberyard won't have stock in the board sizes you've drawn. This is especially true for specialty yards that sell lumber in random lengths and thicknesses. It's frustrating, but it happens. In these situations, you may have to revamp your cutting diagrams right at the lumberyard to work with what's available on the rack. Whatever the case may be, you can always buy more lumber than you need and return what you don't use.

Shopping lists should include more than just lumber and sheet goods. They are good records for logging other items you need for the project, like fasteners, hinges, slide hardware, and glass. Add glue, sandpaper, and finishing supplies to your list too, if you need these items. With luck and a carefully detailed shopping list, you should be able to buy everything you need in just one trip.

A cutting list provides a detailed inventory of all the wood and sheet good parts in the exact sizes that are required to build the project. Use your plan and elevation drawings to list each part, the quantity of that part, and its thickness, width, and length. The list should also identify the wood species or material type for each part. Give each cutting list part a name and letter or number, then go back and label your drawings to match the cutting list naming convention. Now the drawings and cutting list work together to provide all the necessary information you'll need to start building.

Surfacing lumber

If you buy lumber already surfaced on the faces and edges, this may be all the surfacing it needs before use. Inspect each board carefully for straightness before you buy it. Lumber that's kiln-dried and flat at the lumber yard or home center will often stay that way once you've got it stored in your shop, but there's always a chance it may warp, even in the best conditions. When that happens, you may be able to twist the wood flat again just by fastening it to your project or dividing it into smaller, flatter pieces. Eventually you'll encounter a situation where neither of these options will do, and you'll have to do some additional surfacing with hand planes or a power planer and jointer.

Flattening boards with hand planes is a time-honored and respectable skill to learn, but it requires practice and patience. If this sounds like a lot of extra work, surfacing with power tools may be a better option for you. Power jointers and planers smooth and flatten stock in a fraction of the time it takes to do the work by hand, and the learning curve is short.

Machine surfacing is a two-step process, and it requires two tools: a jointer and a planer. The jointer flattens faces and edges, and it makes these surfaces square to

DRAFTING BY COMPUTER

A pencil and paper aren't the only means to create construction drawings, especially if you use a Windows-based PC. Any number of computer assisted drafting (CAD) programs are available for accomplishing the same purpose. CAD software allows you to draw in scale, change the scale as needed and revise your drawings without erasing or starting over. Many have dimensioning tools so you can label your drawings with all the appropriate measurements. Some programs are quite sophisticated, allowing you to render both 2-D and 3-D views, color them with realistic wood tones and even rotate them around as you like. Simpler software packages are inexpensive and usually limit you to making plan and elevation drawings. CAD software is available for Macintosh computers as well as PCs, but the programs tend to be more expensive and there are fewer options to choose from.

Start the surfacing process by flattening one face of a board on the jointer. Use push sticks or push pads to help the stock over the jointer knives and keep your hands clear.

For particularly rough or uneven lumber, you may need to make several passes to flatten the first face. Continue jointing until the face is clean and smooth.

one another. It isn't designed to make opposing faces or edges parallel. Planers keep surfaces parallel, provided one face or edge is already flat. Their primary purposes are smoothing and reducing stock thickness.

Here's how the surfacing process works: Let's assume you have a roughsawn board to surface smooth or a board with minor warp to flatten out. Start by jointing one face flat to create a reference surface. Joint the flatter face whenever possible; you'll save more wood this way by removing just enough of the surface to obtain a flat face. Set the jointer to a cutting depth of $\frac{1}{32}$ inch and adjust the fence so it's square to the jointer bed (the long, horizontal work surface). If your board is wider than 6 or 8 inches, which is the typical maximum cutting width of most home shop jointers, it will be too wide to joint easily. Rip the board so it's narrow enough to joint completely in each pass. (For more on making rip cuts, see pages 63 to 68.)

Hold the board so its face is flat against the jointer bed. Use a push stick or push pad in each hand to keep your fingers and palms safely out of harm's way. Push the board smoothly along the jointer bed and over the spinning knives. Press down on the board evenly as you slide it, shifting more pressure to the jointed side of the board after it passes the knives and less pressure on the portion that still must pass over the knives. Examine the jointed face after the first full pass. If the knives missed some areas, make a few more passes until the entire face makes contact with the knives. Check the face for flatness both lengthwise and widthwise with a long straightedge.

This jointed face becomes a reference surface for smoothing and flattening the other face with the surface planer. Measure the board thickness and set the planer's cutterhead so it will trim the board about $\frac{1}{16}$ inch thinner than it presently is. Deeper passes produce rougher surfaces, dull the planer knives prematurely, and can even stall the motor. For hardwoods, you may need to take an even shallower pass than $\frac{1}{16}$ inch to keep from bogging down the motor. Lock the cutterhead in place if the planer has a locking control for reducing snipe. Feed the board into the machine with the reference face against the smooth planer bed to plane the other face. Drop the cutterhead down another $\frac{1}{16}$ inch if the board needs another pass to smooth the entire face. Now both faces are parallel.

Look closely at the planed face by holding the board up to a light. If the planer is tearing away bits of wood along with smoothing other areas, you're planing against the board's grain direction. Turn the board end for end and try again. This will often correct the tearout problem, but it may not if the board's grain pattern shifts from one direction to the other. When both feed directions produce tearout, try wetting the board with a damp rag to raise the grain, set the machine for shallower passes, and plane the faces again.

Continue the planing process to reduce the board to whatever thickness you need, but keep the thickness at least ¼ inch. Thinner stock becomes flexible, and it can shatter if the board ends get caught in the planer knives. Flip the board from one face to the other with each pass. This practice removes equal amounts of material from both faces, which can help prevent warping.

TIP:

Once you've surfaced some lumber for a project, try to make the parts and assemble them as soon as possible. This way, they'll be straight and true before any additional expansion, contraction, and distortion can take place.

With both board faces planed smooth and parallel, run the board on edge over the jointer to flatten a reference edge. If the jointer fence is square to the bed, the reference edge will be square to both faces. Now the board can be ripped to any width you need. When ripping boards to width on the table saw, be sure to orient the reference edge against the saw's rip fence. This way, the saw will cut an edge parallel to the reference edge.

Resist the urge to plane all your lumber down to a finished thickness as soon as you get it home. A bit of light surfacing can be helpful for assessing the grain patterns and figure of the lumber you have on hand, but keep this surfacing to just a pass or two. Let the wood acclimate to your shop environment in its oversized form until you need to use it. Lumber will need to reach a moisture equilibrium with your shop, and it may distort some in the process as it takes its final shape. Better to allow warping to happen before you've surfaced the lumber to size so you can joint and plane away the distortion. You'll never go wrong starting a project with rough stock that's thicker than you need.

SNIPE

Most power planers will take a slightly deeper bite from the ends of boards when the feed rollers grab or release the lumber as it passes through. This phenomenon is called snipe. Look for shallow dished-out areas usually extending about 2 inches into the board faces. Snipe is difficult to eliminate entirely, and it's not really a sign of a malfunctioning planer. Most manufacturers of portable planers these days outfit their machines with "anti-snipe" locks on the cutterhead to help minimize the problem. The easiest way to contend with snipe is to do your planing on stock about 4 to 6 inches longer than you need, then trim off the sniped portions after surfacing. If the snipe is minimal, just sand these areas to blend them in to the rest of the board face. Jointers are capable of producing snipe, too, but generally you can fix this by adjusting the jointer beds and cutterhead.

Chapter 4
PREPARING PARTS

Once you've drafted a set of measured drawings, itemized a cutting list, and bought the necessary lumber and sheet materials, the next step is part-making. For most woodworkers, here's where the real fun starts! Preparing parts begins with careful stock layout, based on the dimensions you've determined in the cutting list. After parts are measured and marked, you'll cut them to rough size, then refine the proportions with more cutting, routing, and sanding.

Layout

Laying out workpieces for a project is equal parts mental gymnastics and line drawing. The task involves three activities: planning how to divvy up your building materials efficiently, measuring the part sizes, and penciling them to shape. Since you'll draw each part to full size, careful layout work will literally show you if you've bought enough material to make all the parts on your cutting list. It's also a chance to strategize the best arrangement of parts on each board so you can cut them out easily and minimize waste. Now is also the time to select boards with the best figure and grain pattern for parts you'll want to highlight on your project, while leaving less desirable wood for pieces that won't show.

Three approaches to part layout. There are three schools of thought on how to lay out parts. Many woodworking project books and magazines advocate laying out all the parts at once and cutting them to size, one after the next. All the layout work happens at the beginning of a project. The main advantage to this method is efficiency. Marking all the parts to size, then cutting them

LAYOUT TOOLS

A few key tools will provide most of what you'll need for the usual layout tasks. Here are the ones to keep on hand:

- No. 2 pencils or carpenter's pencils
- White colored pencil (for dark woods)
- Tape measure (10 feet or longer)
- Combination square with 12-inch or longer blade
- Framing square
- Bevel gauge
- 3- or 4-foot straightedge
- Chalk line
- 8-in. compass
- Try square

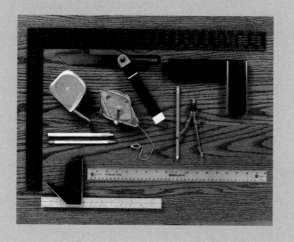

out in one fell swoop takes care of part-making in a hurry. The downside to this method is it leaves you precious little margin for error. Once the boards are cut to size, you can't change your mind about the details or proportions of the project. You're committed to the design as is. If mistakes happen in the building process, you may have to remake some parts entirely rather than modify other part sizes to account for the mistake. While it's admittedly satisfying to make neat stacks of parts and complete this first building step, avoid this approach until you're confident with your project designs and part-making skills.

Another option is to lay out and cut parts in stages as you work through your project. Layout becomes a task that happens from the beginning of the construction process to nearly the end. For example, if you're building a table with a drawer, you might lay out and cut the legs, aprons, and other parts that form the table's base, then mill the joinery and assemble the base before moving on to the tabletop. After building the tabletop, more layout and cutting would produce the drawer components. The upside to this approach is that you can make changes as the building process unfolds. It's an especially forgiving method for working through those inevitable mistakes. If the tabletop looks too small or the drawer needs to be a bit wider than you planned in your construction drawings, you can change the proportions before laying out and cutting the parts.

A third layout technique, which is really a hybrid of the first two approaches, is to lay out and cut all the parts on your cutting list at the beginning, but make them a few inches longer and wider than necessary. This approach works well for large projects with long cutting lists that require lots of lumber. Sometimes it helps to size those stacks of boards down into smaller pieces immediately to get them off the floor and out of your way. Once the parts are cut to oversize proportions, you'll also know if you have enough material for all the parts you need. Occasionally, boards will warp after they are cut up. If the parts are larger than final size, you can correct for minor warpage at the rough size stage, then trim the parts to final size. The drawback to this approach is that cutting everything oversize produces more waste.

Whichever layout method you choose, the process of arranging parts on a board really depends on the types of parts you need to make and the sizes of lumber you have on hand. Here are some general guidelines to keep in mind as you work through the layout process:

• Spread out your boards and select the straightest or most attractive stock first. Start by marking the parts that need to be made from prime material. Usually these parts include drawer faces, panels for doors or table tops, face frame rails and stiles, and any other pieces that should take advantage of interesting or matching grain pattern and figure.

• Don't feel obligated to work your way down the cutting list, laying out and cutting each part in order. Instead, try to keep the overall cutting list in mind, but arrange parts on boards in ways that use the lumber efficiently. If, for instance, you have a 27-inch-long part and a 30-inch-long part to make, look for a board around 5 feet to lay out both parts. A 6-foot board could work too, but you'd end up with 1 foot of lumber in the scrap bin unless you have some smaller parts to use it for. This might mean that Part A fits next to Part M on your board layout, which is fine.

• As you measure and mark parts onto each board, label them according to the cutting list. Parts without labels are easy to confuse once you've cut them. Mark each part label on both a face and an edge or end. More than likely, you'll machine away at least one of these labels, but the other label usually stays intact. At some point, parts become unmistakable as you machine them to shape. Until that time comes, re-label parts as needed to keep things clear.

Before laying out project parts, separate your lumber by quality. Reserve the prime material for parts that will show. Try to match grain patterns if you're making wide panels. Cut up less desirable lumber into smaller parts.

• Use a permanent marker or carpenter's pencil with a heavy lead to label the parts. These identifiers should be easy to read and tough to rub off. Masking tape also works, but cheap tape can be difficult to peel off once the adhesive sets on the wood.

• Solid lumber is strongest along the grain. Make the longest dimension of any part follow the grain direction on a board. Oftentimes the part shape will make this grain direction issue obvious. Rectangular parts may only fit on a board if you plot them out to follow the grain direction. For shorter or more square-shaped parts, where the grain direction could be plotted to go either way, let the visual cues of the project dictate grain direction. If the part will need some form of interlocking joint cut into the ends, mill the joints in long-grain material. Short-grain joints form weaker connections and tend to break easily.

• When cutting parts from long boards or heavy, unwieldy sheets of plywood, lay out the material in such a way that one or two cuts will size it down into more manageable workpieces. A quarter sheet of plywood is easier to lift onto a workbench or feed through a table saw than a full sheet.

Tenons, rabbets, tongues, and dovetails should be cut from long-grain material whenever possible.

For plotting out parts, you'll need a tape measure, a straightedge, and a square. If parts have angles other than 45° or 90°, you'll also need a bevel gauge to scribe the correct angle. Use a sharp pencil to make crisp reference lines, and resharpen the pencil frequently as it dulls.

Most parts in a conventional woodworking project have at least one flat edge or end and typically a square corner. When drawing a part to shape, work from its flat edge or square corner to lay it out. On plywood and other sheet goods, the factory edges and ends of the sheets are generally reliably flat and square. For boards, use the reference edge you flattened on a jointer. If you didn't use a jointer to form flat edges, select the flattest manufactured edges to lay out your parts.

USING A SQUARE

Squares are invaluable layout tools for drawing perpendicular lines. Hold the head of the square against a flat edge or end of a workpiece, and scribe along the blade to mark a square corner. Combination squares offer the added benefit of both 45° and 90° angles on the head for drawing either of these line angles. The blades of most squares are outfitted with rulers, so the tools double

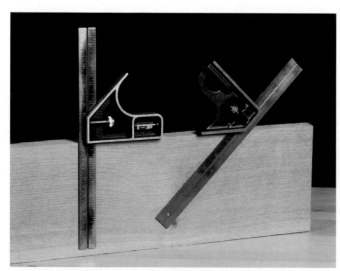

If you buy just one square for woodworking, make it a combination square. The head sets the rule for scribing either 90° or 45° angles, depending on how you set the square on a workpiece.

You can also use a combination square for drawing accurate lines parallel to a board edge. Hold a pencil against the end of the rule and drag the square and rule along the board together.

as measuring devices. The square's head forms a solid starting point for "zero distance" to plot line lengths. If you need to draw a line parallel to the edge of a workpiece, lock the blade of a combination square so the end matches the distance you want between the parallel line and the board edge. Hold a pencil against the end of the blade, and slide the pencil and square together along the board edge to draw the parallel line.

Try squares have heads that are permanently fixed to the blade. They can be used like combination squares for marking square corners, although the rules are generally shorter. All-metal try squares are handy for checking machine fences for square. They're often called engineering squares and calibrated to higher degree of accuracy than try squares with wooden heads.

Use a framing square for drawing larger square corners. Framing squares are generally less accurate than smaller try or combination squares, but they work fine for marking parts to rough size. The 4-foot T-style squares used for marking drywall are also useful here; they have a flat ledge along the "T" for registering the tool in position, and the blade is long enough to reach across the width of a full sheet of plywood. Be aware that these squares aren't engineered for high precision. Check yours by holding it against a known square corner to see if it holds a true 90°.

Bevel gauges can be adjusted to any angle using a protractor as a reference. They're also helpful tools for matching an unknown angle and transferring it precisely to another tool or workpiece.

USING A BEVEL GAUGE

Bevel gauges are really just squares with adjustable blades. A bevel gauge can be locked to any angle by tightening the nut at the base of the blade. Bevel gauges make wonderful duplicating devices in layout work. In cases where you don't know the measure of an angle but need to transfer it to another surface, a bevel gauge takes out the calculation work. Hold the head of the tool against one reference surface and adjust and lock the blade to match the angle you're transferring. If you need to create an angled line with a specific degree of measure, set the gauge with a protractor. Hold the bevel gauge stock against the protractor's flat reference edge, and align the blade edge with the center of the protractor. Pivot the blade to match the protractor angle you need, then lock the bevel.

USING A TAPE MEASURE

A tape measure is indispensable for rough layout work. To plot part lengths, hook the tape's clip over a reference edge, extend the tape, and mark the distance you need. Measuring off the end of a tape is accurate enough for general layout tasks, but once parts are cut to rough size, switch to a modified approach for taking fine measurements. Instead of measuring off the clip, use the 1-inch mark as your starting point. The moveable clip makes the first inch a less precise unit of measure than the others. When starting from the 1-inch mark, remember to subtract 1 inch from the overall measurement indicated on the tape to determine the actual distance—as is, you're offset by 1 inch.

For better accuracy, measure beginning at the 1-inch mark on a tape measure, then subtract 1 inch from the measured distance.

If you don't own a long metal rule, use the factory edge on a piece of sheet material as a surrogate straightedge for scribing long, straight lines.

PLOTTING LONG LINES WITH A CHALK LINE OR STRAIGHTEDGE

One way to mark long layout lines on large sheets of plywood or wide boards is to use a chalk line. Mark reference points on each end of the line you want to plot, then stretch the chalk line and hold it against the reference marks. Stretch the string taut from one end and hold it against both reference marks. Pull the string up, like drawing the string on a bow, and let it snap back. The string will leave a straight chalked line in its place on the workpiece.

You can also use a long metal straightedge or even a piece of straight scrap wood to draw long layout lines. Make a series of reference marks with a tape measure to mark the path of the layout line. Connect the marks with the straightedge and a pencil.

DRAWING CIRCLES & CURVES

For circles with radii less than 8 inches, use a compass to scribe the shape. Spread the legs of the compass to the correct radius measurement and lock the setting. Push the sharpened tip into the workpiece to register the circle's centerpoint, and swing the compass pencil around the tip to draw the shape. For larger circles, mount a pair of trammel points to a piece of scrap wood and draw the circle this way. The trammel points slide to any position along the scrap and tighten in place with set screws to establish the circle's radius. One trammel can be outfitted with a pencil, like a compass. The other trammel has a metal tip. Swinging the scrap and pencil trammel around the trammel with the metal tip draws the circle.

To make curved but non-circular shapes, you'll have to be a bit more resourceful. Art and drafting supply stores sell French curves, which provide a template of different curvatures for making smaller curves. You can also buy flexible curves from woodworking suppliers that are made of lead and bendable to any curved shape. A length of heavy-gauge electrical wire works just as well. Mold the wire into the curve you need, and use it as a template.

A pair of trammel points attached to a strip of wood enable you to draw circles of any size.

Hardboard, also known as Masonite, is invaluable for making durable, reusable templates. If you plan to build more than one of the same project, save those templates!

When measuring and marking part shapes, it's just as easy to draw the wrong line as the right one. One easy way to keep layout errors from becoming cutting errors is to doublecheck your work and keep your layouts tidy. The old, overused adage, "Measure twice, cut once," is really a good rule to follow. Erase incorrect cutting lines and non-essential layout lines as soon as you make them rather than marking them with Xs, scribbling them out, or making mental notes of what lines not to follow. It only takes a moment's lapse in concentration to cut along the wrong line, so keep only those lines necessary for making the part. Draw your pencil lines lightly so they're easy to erase or wipe away with a damp rag.

When you need to scribe a smooth arch, a long narrow strip of hardboard or a thin scrap of solid wood produces a smooth shape when flexed and held between a few nails tacked along the curve.

USING TEMPLATES

If you have more than two matching parts to make, especially if they're oddly shaped, you'll speed the layout process and avoid measurement errors by tracing the shape off a template. For a particularly crucial part, you may want to make a template to help make just this part. Hardboard is a durable and inexpensive material for making templates, although scrap wood, posterboard, and even heavy paper will work too. With a template as your pattern, you can be certain that parts will be exactly the same size.

Making basic cuts

Cutting out parts requires six types of cuts: rip cuts, crosscuts, angled cuts, curved cuts, profile cuts, and template cuts. Generally, stationary power tools produce cleaner cuts than handheld power tools, but you can do respectable work with a circular saw or jig saw if you're careful and use the right jig or accessory.

The common understanding of rip cutting, or ripping, is to cut parallel with the grain pattern. This definition is more accurate for cutting solid wood than plywood, which doesn't have a consistent grain pattern running through its thickness. Either way, rip cuts commonly form the width of a workpiece.

Rip cutting with a table saw: Table saws are well-suited for rip cutting, and they're probably used for this purpose more than for making any other type of cut. A table saw has a long rip fence oriented parallel with the saw blade that stretches across the saw table. It can be positioned any distance from the blade and locked for ripping purposes. Making rip cuts involves feeding workpieces through the blade and against the rip fence, pushing the wood with your hands or with push

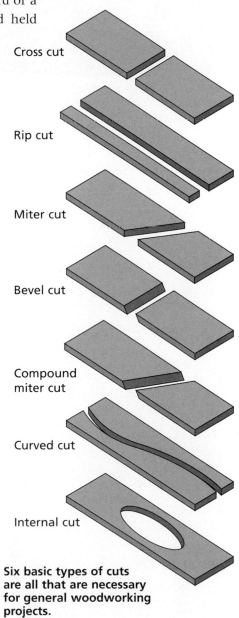

Cross cut

Rip cut

Miter cut

Bevel cut

Compound miter cut

Curved cut

Internal cut

Six basic types of cuts are all that are necessary for general woodworking projects.

Table saws are well-suited for making rip cuts. The rip fence keeps workpieces parallel to the blade and establishes the width of what you're cutting.

sticks when the material is narrow. The saw's broad table provides good support for workpieces, but generally you'll want to add more support behind the machine when cutting particularly long boards to catch the pieces and keep them from tipping off the table. A work table, roller stand, or even a tall saw horse is a good support option behind a table saw. The outfeed device should be about ¼ inch shorter than the saw's table to keep workpieces from catching on it as they leave the saw.

One inherent danger of using a table saw for ripping is that boards can bind between the rip fence and the blade. Another danger is that the cutting channel created by the blade (called the kerf) can close up around the blade. In either of these scenarios, if the blade teeth catch the wood, they will lift the workpiece off the table and fling it back in your direction forcefully and at great speed. This situation is called kickback, and it's the leading cause of table saw-related accidents. The way to avoid kickback is to install the guard and splitter assembly that comes with your saw and use it every time you make rip cuts. Be sure that your saw's rip fence is parallel with the saw blade, and the blade is clean and sharp.

Here's how to make rip cuts with a table saw: First, adjust the rip fence so the distance between the fence and the closest face of the saw blade equals the workpiece width you want to cut. Lock the fence in place. With the saw unplugged, set the workpiece on the saw table and raise the blade so the teeth project above the wood all the way to the bottom of the gullets (the curved cutouts between the teeth). This height generally produces cleaner cuts than setting the blade lower in the work, and it's safer than exposing even more blade.

To make the cut, stand to the left of the workpiece. When cutting shorter lumber, touch your left foot to the front left corner of the saw base, if you are close enough to reach it. This stance will help you maintain your balance during the cut. Start the saw and rest the workpiece on the saw table in front of the blade. Press the workpiece against the rip fence while slowly sliding it forward until it engages the blade teeth. Once the blade "kisses" the board, feed it into the blade with your right hand and hold the board against the rip fence with your left hand. Feed the workpiece as quickly and smoothly through the blade as you can without causing the motor to labor or stall. Maintain forward motion at all times. If the motor starts to bog down, slow your feed rate so the blade can build up to full speed again. When the back end of the board reaches the saw table, use a push stick in your right hand to feed the board the rest of the way past the blade. Hold a second push stick in your left hand to keep the work tight against the fence. Stop feeding with the left push stick when the end of the board approaches the blade. Once the board slices in two and the right portion is clear of the blade, slide the wastepiece away from the blade with the left push stick. If the scrap is small or narrow, shut off the saw and wait until the blade stops before removing the scrap.

CAUTION: Never allow your hands to come within 6 inches of a spinning table saw blade for any reason. Use a push stick instead.

Ripping sheet materials with a table saw: You can rip full-size sheets of plywood or other composite material with a table saw using essentially the same ripping procedure as for solid lumber. The challenge is to maintain control of these unwieldy and sometimes heavy sheet materials while feeding them through the saw. Provide some means of sturdy workpiece support behind the saw to bear the weight. A work table or a pair of roller stands set just lower than the saw table height make good support devices. When ripping wide sheet goods you may also want to position workpiece support alongside the saw. If the proportions or weight of your sheet material make the ripping process seem too daunting at the table saw, use a circular saw instead.

Rip cutting with a circular saw: A circular saw outfitted with a general-purpose carbide-tipped blade makes a fine ripping tool for less exacting applications. Circular saws tend to produce more splintering around the cut edges than table saws, but they can be safer than table saws for rough-cutting large workpieces. Circular saws should only be used for ripping when workpieces are wider than the saw base. Otherwise, the saw will be tippy and difficult to control.

PUSH STICKS & PUSH PADS

Push sticks are plastic or wood safety devices used to keep your hands clear of bits and blades on stationary power tools. They're typically shaped like a long handle with a bird's mouth cut in one end to hold workpieces securely. Some look more like paddles with a long sole on the bottom. Push pads serve the same purpose as push sticks, but they have a handle mounted to a flat pad that's typically covered with foam rubber to keep the pad from slipping. Keep a pair of these safety devices within arm's reach of your table saw, jointer, and router table at all times. You can buy inexpensive push sticks anywhere woodworking tools and supplies are sold or make them yourself from scrap wood. Use push sticks and push pads instead of your hands whenever you're working within 6 inches of a blade or bit. When ripping narrow strips of lumber between the rip fence and blade, use a push stick that's thinner than the cutting width of the workpieces. Hardboard push sticks work well in these situations.

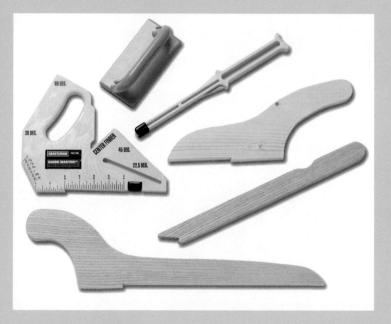

CHOOSING A TABLE SAW BLADE

A good all-around blade to keep in your saw is one intended for "general purpose" or "combination" use. These blades usually have 40 or 50 carbide-tipped teeth configured to make smooth rip and crosscuts in hardwoods, softwoods, and sheet goods. If you do a significant amount of ripping, consider buying a dedicated ripping blade. These blades usually have 18 to 36 large, flat-topped teeth designed for faster material feeding. Crosscutting blades have 60 to 80 or more teeth and make glass-smooth cross-grain cuts, but the high tooth count makes for slow ripping. Unless you do a lot of crosscutting, a specialized crosscut blade probably isn't worth the extra money. If you need to cut melamine, veneered plywood, plastic, or non-ferrous metal, specialized blades are available for these purposes too.

Circular saws pose the same kickback hazard as table saws if the blade gets pinched while cutting. Avoid kickback by following a couple easy preventive measures. First, keep your circular saw blade clean by removing pitch and other deposits with spray-on blade cleaner. Dirty blades bind more easily than clean blades. Set the blade depth so the teeth project ¼ to ½ inch below the workpiece. Provide plenty of support beneath your workpiece to keep it from sagging and binding the blade, which can lead to kickback. If the saw kerf begins to close up behind the tool—a common problem when cutting solid wood—insert a wedge in the kerf to spread it open again before proceeding with the cut.

For ripping situations where accuracy isn't critical, you can guide a circular saw freehand along a cutting line. In most woodworking situations, you'll want more control and precision than "eyeballing" your rip cuts. Clamp a straight piece of scrap lumber or a metal straightedge firmly to your workpiece to form a makeshift rip fence, and run the edge of the saw base against the straightedge. You'll need to offset the straightedge from your cutting line to account for the saw base width. Find the amount of offset by measuring from the edge of the base to the blade teeth.

Another way to make rip cuts with a circular saw is to use the adjustable ripping guide that comes with most saws. It resembles a "T" and fits on the saw like an out-

One method of making accurate rip cuts with a circular saw is to guide the saw base against a straightedge clamped in place.

rigger. Clamp it to the front of the saw base so the bearing surface of the guide will ride against the edge of the workpiece. When using this guide, set up the cut so the wider side of the saw base rests on the portion of the workpiece that won't be cut free. Always try to keep the wider side of the base planted on a stable surface. When making the rip cut, keep tension on the fence by pulling the saw toward you as you push the saw forward and through the cut. This will keep the saw from wandering off the cutting line.

Rip cutting with jig saws and band saws: Jig saws and band saws are safer power tools to use for making rip cuts than table saws or circular saws. Because the blades cut in an in-line rather than circular motion, they don't produce the rotational forces that lead to kickback. These blades also cut thinner kerfs, which reduce the amount of wasted wood. Both jigsaws and band saws can make curved as well as straight cuts, unlike circular saws or table saws that are limited to just straight cuts. However, jig saws and band saws make rip cuts more slowly than saws with circular blades.

Another option for making rip cuts close to the edge of a workpiece is to install a ripping guide on the saw base. Make the cut with the bearing surface of the guide riding along the workpiece edge.

Rip-cutting with a jig saw is done by guiding the tool freehand or against a clamped straightedge, like a circular saw. Jig saw blades are quite narrow and only supported from above the cut, so they tend to flex and wander a bit when cutting thick material. For fast rip cuts, choose a wide blade with a low number

CHOOSING A CIRCULAR SAW BLADE

Most ordinary circular saws accept 7¼-inch diameter blades, and there are many to choose from. For general ripping, blades with fewer teeth cut more quickly but make rougher edges. "Combination" blades with between 16 and 24 teeth do a good job of ripping and crosscutting most woods. Choose a

blade outfitted with antikickback shoulders. These small humps behind the teeth limit the amount of material each tooth can remove.

Most circular saw blades now have thinner blade bodies than table saw blades, so they cut a narrower kerf and require less energy from the tool during cutting. Look for a "thin kerf" designation on the package. When cutting splintery materials such as plywood, or melamine and particleboard that are prone to chipping, switch to a blade intended for cutting plywood. These blades have scores of small teeth that take tiny bites of material. You'll have to feed the tool more slowly, but the smaller teeth produce virtually splinter-free edges.

of teeth per inch. The blade will have large teeth and gullets. Thicker blades will
help reduce flexing, too.

Band saws cut more smoothly than jig saws. You'll also have improved control
over the cut. A band saw blade is held under tension both above and below the
cutting surface, so it tends to cut square, clean edges if properly adjusted. Band
saws are also better choices than jig saws for ripping narrow stock; it's easier to
feed a narrow workpiece through the blade than to work the other way
around, moving the tool over the wood.

For ripping, choose a wide skip-tooth band saw blade. It cuts more quickly and
cleanly than narrower blades with more teeth. Make the cut by feeding the
work freehand through the blade and following your cutting line by eye. For
more accuracy, you can also use a rip fence or straight piece of scrap clamped

to the saw table and feed the work into the blade like
you would for making rip cuts on a table saw. If the
blade wanders off the cut when using a rip fence, you
may need to adjust the fence so it's slightly skewed to
the blade. This phenomenon is called blade drift, and it's
a common problem with band saws.

CROSSCUTS

As the name suggests, crosscutting involves cutting solid
wood across the grain. Rip cuts establish the width of a
workpiece, and a pair of crosscuts set the length. The
common definition of crosscutting implies that these
cuts are square to the board edges, although angled
cross-grain cuts are technically crosscuts as well. Any
tool capable of making rip cuts can be used for crosscutting, but the more accurate tools for this operation are
the table saw, power miter saw, radial arm saw, and
circular saw.

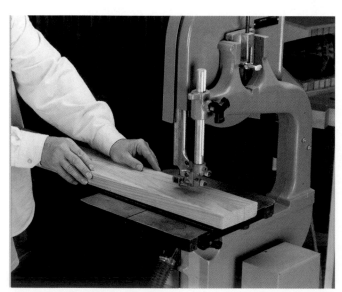

Band saws make both straight and curved rip cuts with
equal ease. You can guide the cuts freehand or against a
rip fence clamped in place.

Crosscutting with a table saw: For crosscutting on a table saw, use a miter gauge. Miter gauges are standard equipment on virtually every brand of table saw. They consist of a protractor-style head attached to a metal bar that slides in a pair of slots on either side of the saw blade. When set to 0°, the miter gauge forms a 90° angle relative to the blade.

The procedure for making a crosscut with a miter gauge is easy: Hold a workpiece against the miter gauge fence so the cutting line on the workpiece aligns with the saw blade. (Check for alignment by sliding the workpiece up to the blade with the saw turned off.) Turn on the saw and slide the gauge and workpiece together across the saw table and past the blade. Be sure to slide the rip fence out of the way of both the workpiece and the wastepiece before making the cut so it doesn't make contact with the material on either side of the blade.

Making crosscuts with a table saw involves the use of a miter gauge. The device supports workpieces from behind and slides in a pair of slots cut in the saw table.

CAUTION: It is never safe to make crosscuts using the rip fence instead of the miter gauge. The rip fence does not support workpieces from behind like miter gauges do. Workpieces crosscut against the rip fence tend to veer off the fence, bind the blade, and kick back. It is also not safe to hold workpieces against both the miter gauge and the rip fence during crosscutting. Although the rip fence would seem to make a handy stop for cutting workpieces to the same length, it actually can trap them between the blade and miter gauge, leading to kickback.

CROSSCUT SLEDS

Many professional woodworkers use crosscut sleds instead of miter gauges for crosscutting. A crosscut sled is simply a sheet of plywood with a tall fence along either edge mounted to a couple runners that fit in both miter slots. A saw kerf divides the middle of the sled in two to provide a clear track for the blade. Plans for building crosscut sleds are available in many woodworking project books and appear as project stories in woodworking magazines from time to time.

Using the jig involves placing workpieces inside the sled and against the back fence, then sliding the sled across the table to make the cut. Crosscut sleds provide several advantages over miter gauges. By holding workpieces stationary and sliding the sled, you keep the wood from moving laterally during cutting, so cuts are much more precise. The sled fence provides a backing surface behind workpieces to help minimize splintering. Once the fence is set perpendicular to the saw blade, it never needs readjustment to make perfect square cuts.

If the bar on your miter gauge fits loosely in the miter slots, tap a series of dimples along the edges of the bar with a with a nail set or metal punch. The resulting dimples will improve the fit.

Miter gauges are capable of making fairly precise crosscuts on workpieces up to a couple feet in length. However, several adjustments and simple improvements will boost their accuracy and performance significantly. First, hold the stock of a combination or try square against the fence of your miter gauge and adjust the miter head until the square's blade is flush against the miter bar. If your miter gauge has an adjustable flip-up stop for 0°, set it here after checking for square.

Notice that the fence on your miter gauge is less than 6 or 8 inches long. As is, it is too short to provide adequate support behind longer workpieces. Remedy the problem by attaching a flat scrap of wood or sheet goods material about 16 to 24 inches long and 3 or 4 inches wide to your miter fence with short screws. This forms an auxiliary wood fence. Then glue a strip of medium-grit sandpaper to the face. Position the auxiliary fence on the miter fence so the end near the blade stops just short of the blade guard. With this added bearing surface, you'll be able to crosscut longer workpieces, and the sandpaper will keep them from creeping away from the blade during cutting.

Another way to help your miter gauge cut more accurately is to minimize a sloppy fit in the miter slots. Set the gauge in a miter slot and try to jiggle it from side to side. If the bar moves in the slot, this extra play will result in rough crosscuts. To improve the fit, tap a series of dimples along the edges of the bar using a nail set and hammer. The dimples provide a bit of extra metal to fill the gap in the miter slot. File down the dimples slightly if the fit goes from being too loose to too tight. Ideally, the gauge should slide smoothly but without any noticeable side-to-side play. If you have a newer or aftermarket miter gauge on your saw, it may have expansion screws or adjustable disks along the miter bar to take up extra play.

Crosscutting with a power miter saw: Power miter saws look like hybrid circular saws mounted on a swiveling base. The motor and blade plunge downward and into a kerf slot in the base to make a cut. For making angled cuts, bases turn left and right to adjust the blade relative to a fence on the tool. Compound miter saws have a control arm that tips the motor and blade left or right for cutting bevels. Some saws slide back and forth on tubes, which expands their crosscutting capacity. Miter saws are sized by the maximum blade diameter they accept. Sizes range from about 7 inches up to 14 inches.

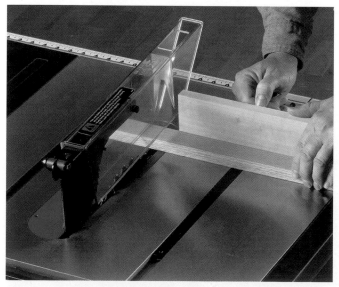

The fence on a miter gauge is often too small to support larger workpieces adequately. Add more bearing support by attaching a larger wood fence to the miter gauge with screws.

Of all the crosscutting machines, power miter saws are arguably the most accurate. With the appropriate crosscutting blade, these handy saws are engineered to make glass-smooth crosscuts that need no further finishing work. Their primary limitation is width of cut. Large plunge-style miter saws offer a maximum crosscutting capacity of about 10 inches. Sliding miter saws can cut wider workpieces, but they're still limited by the travel length of the motor carriage.

Making crosscuts with either a plunge-style or sliding miter saw is a straightforward operation. For a plunge saw, set the workpiece snug against the fence on the saw base so the cutting line is even with the blade. Check for alignment by pivoting the blade down against the workpiece with the saw turned off. Be sure to register the cut so the blade is on the waste side of the cutting line. If the workpiece is long enough to keep your hands outside the danger zone designated on the tool, you can hold the wood against the tool by hand. Use a push stick to hold shorter workpieces against the fence or a holddown clamp if your saw has one. Make the cut by turning on the saw and gently pushing the blade down through the workpiece. Once the saw drops to its full cutting range, release the motor trigger and let the blade stop before raising the blade out of the workpiece.

The cutting procedure for a sliding miter saw is a bit different than for a plunge saw. Pull the motor carriage toward you and lower the blade onto the workpiece to check for blade alignment. Raise the blade all the way up and start the saw. Lower the blade down into the saw base kerf, and push the motor carriage away from you to make the cut. Wait until the blade stops before withdrawing it from the workpiece.

When using either saw type, it's a good idea to clamp or bolt the saw base securely to a work surface before cutting. This is especially true for sliding miter saws with narrow bases. The sliding motion can shift the machine's center of gravity and cause it to tip backward during a cut. If you're cutting particularly long workpieces, you may also need to provide additional support alongside the tool to keep the wood from tipping off the saw table after it's cut.

Crosscutting with a circular saw: For the occasional "quick and dirty" crosscut, a circular saw is a good choice. Use the same blade depth settings as for rip cuts. When accuracy isn't critical, simply guide the saw freehand to make the cut. Clamp a straightedge across the workpiece for cutting more accurately. Contractors often use a speed square with a flared base as a jobsite crosscutting fence. Hold the square against the workpiece so the flare fits over an edge. Position the saw base against the square, and adjust both until the saw blade lines up with the cutting line on the workpiece. Slide the saw along the square to make the cut.

TIP: Before making crosscuts with a power miter saw, tune the blade so it is square to both the saw base and the fence. Use a square held against the blade body—not the teeth—to check both of these positions. All saws have adjustment screws for fine-tuning blade and fence alignment. The owner's manual will outline the tuning process. Once these adjustments are made, the saw should hold blade and fence settings permanently unless the tool is transported often or damaged in some way. Check the blade and fence settings occasionally just to be sure.

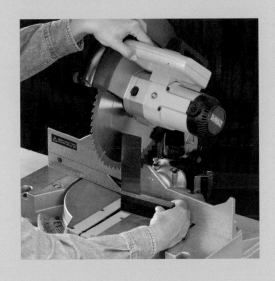

Guide a circular saw against the blade of a speed square to improve the tool's accuracy when making crosscuts.

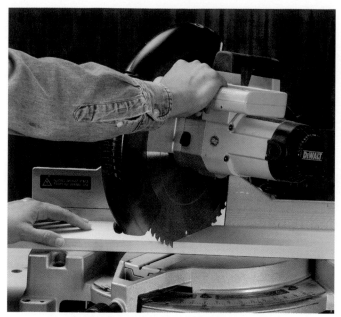

Making a crosscut with a plunge-style miter saw involves holding the workpiece against the saw fence and pivoting the spinning blade down into it.

Crosscutting with a sliding miter saw is a little different. Here, you pull the saw carriage forward, lower the spinning blade into the workpiece, and push the carriage back through the wood.

Crosscutting with a radial arm saw: Radial arm saws work in reverse of sliding miter saws. The motor and blade ride along a carriage above the saw table, but with this machine, you pull the motor toward you during a cut rather than push it away. The blade maintains the same cutting depth throughout the cut instead of pivoting. Radial arm saws are especially useful for crosscutting long, heavy workpieces. They can also be outfitted with dado blades for cutting wide grooves for joinery.

To make a crosscut, slide the motor carriage away from you and position the workpiece against the saw's fence. Line up the cut with the motor off, then push the carriage back so the blade is clear of the fence and workpiece. Start the saw and slowly pull the motor carriage toward you until the blade cuts the workpiece in two. Release the trigger and allow the blade to stop before removing the workpiece sections and sliding the saw carriage back to the starting position. Use hand pressure or push sticks to hold workpieces against the fence.

CAUTION: Use extreme care when advancing the motor and blade through the cut. Feeding the blade too rapidly into a cut can cause the blade to climb up over the workpiece and propel itself with great force in your direction. Always keep a firm grip on the motor handle during the entire cut.

ANGLED CUTS

There are two types of angled cuts to make when preparing parts: miters and bevels. These terms are used somewhat carelessly from time to time in books and magazines, so much so that it can be difficult to keep their differences clear. Miters are angled cuts across the face of a workpiece with the saw blade positioned perpendicular to the saw table or tool base. Bevel-cutting involves cutting the edges or ends of a workpiece with the blade tipped to some angle other than 90°.

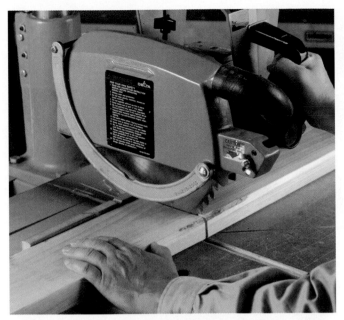

Radial-arm saws function in the reverse of sliding miter saws for making crosscuts. Start the blade and pull it toward you and through the workpiece. Be sure to hold the workpiece firmly against the fence on the saw table.

Pivot and lock the miter gauge head at an angle for making miter cuts. Attaching an auxiliary fence to the miter gauge provides additional support, and a stop block clamped in place keeps the workpiece from shifting along the fence during the cut.

Cutting miters and bevels with a table saw: Not surprisingly, miter cutting on a table saw is done with the miter gauge. This time, the protractor head of the gauge is swiveled and locked to a non-square setting. The cutting procedure is the same as for making crosscuts, but it's particularly important to hold workpieces tightly against the miter gauge fence. The workpiece will be particularly prone to shifting.

Cutting bevels with a table saw involves tilting the blade to some angle other than 90°. Saws usually allow bevel settings up to 45°. When you're beveling an edge, use the rip fence to support the workpiece as you push it through the blade. Always orient the rip fence on the side of the saw table opposite the direction of blade tilt. If the blade tips right, slide the fence to the left of the blade. This way, workpieces can't get trapped between the rip fence and the tipped blade, where they can catch on the blade teeth and kick back.

For beveling the ends of workpieces, hold the part against the miter gauge with the fence set to 0°. Keep the rip fence clear, just like crosscutting. Set up these bevel cuts so the portion of a workpiece that's cut free doesn't end up on top of the spinning blade where it can get caught and thrown from the saw table. Hold the longer portion of the workpiece against the miter gauge. Once the cut is made, the cutoff piece will fall away below the blade.

When making beveled cuts using the rip fence, set the fence on the side of the saw opposite the direction the blade tilts. Cutoffs should fall away from the blade and below it, not rest on top of the blade.

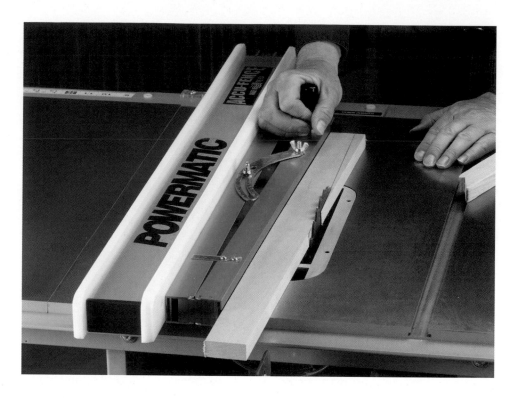

Ripping tapers: Tapers are rip cuts that follow the long grain but cut the edge of a board at an angle. You'll see tapers used most commonly on table or chair legs, and generally the legs will be tapered on two adjacent edges. Tapers are an attractive way to slim down the proportions of furniture parts, and they're easy to cut on a table saw using a simple tapering jig. Do not attempt to cut tapers by holding a workpiece at an angle to the blade without anchoring it in a jig. There's no way to accurately make a freehand cut, and the wood will probably kick back in the process.

Tapering jigs are inexpensive and easy to use, or you can build your own. Fabricated tapering jigs consist of two adjustable "arms" joined by a hinge on one end. One arm rides against the rip fence and the other arm holds the workpiece at an angle to the blade. A stop on the end of the workpiece arm steadies the workpiece as you slide the jig and workpiece past the blade. There is also an adjustable brace spanning both arms that locks the arms at whatever taper angle you choose.

One drawback to the two-arm-style tapering jig is that it doesn't have a feature that holds the workpiece tight against the arm while you cut the taper. For tapers that don't run the length of a workpiece, it's a good idea to clamp the workpiece to the arm outside the cutting area. For full-length taper cuts, use a push stick to steady the workpiece against the jig as best you can.

Here's how to set up for cutting tapers with an adjustable jig: Mark the workpiece with layout lines showing the tapered edge. Use a straightedge and pencil to draw a line across the front of the saw table that shows the exact path of the saw blade. Set the straightedge against the side of the blade closest to the rip fence to mark this line. Place the tapering jig against the rip fence and the workpiece in the jig. Adjust the arm that holds the workpiece until the line you made on the workpiece aligns with the blade reference line on the table. Slide the rip fence closer to the blade, if necessary, to help align the jig. Using a reference line on the saw table, you'll know exactly where the blade will cut the workpiece. Lock the jig arms and rip fence to hold their positions.

Back the jig up to the front of the table so the workpiece clears the blade. To cut the taper, slide the jig and workpiece along the fence as you would a normal rip cut. If you'd like to cut a matching taper on an adjacent edge, flip the workpiece in the jig so the first taper faces up, then cut the second taper. To taper all four faces, reset the jig for twice the first angle after you've cut two tapered edges; at this point you'll need to rest a tapered edge against the adjustable arm, which is why the jig must be set to twice the initial angle.

Cutting miters and bevels with a power miter saw: Making miter cuts with a power miter saw is a simple matter of swiveling the saw base to the correct miter angle, resting the workpiece against the fence and base, and making the cut. Miter saws have preset detents (stops) for cutting the more common framing angles, such as 22.5°, 30°, and 45°. The saw base will snap positively into these stops when you release a lever near the front tension knob. If you need to cut a less common angle, position the scale's cursor carefully, then tighten the tension knob to lock the base. Cut the miter just as you would a square crosscut.

Not all miter saws can be adjusted to cut bevel angles, but most newer units can. When a saw can cut bevels as well as miters, it's called a compound miter saw. The beveling feature allows the motor head to tip so the blade meets the saw table at different vertical angles. A scale on the motor arm of the machine indicates the degree of bevel tilt, and a lock knob holds the blade at whatever angle you need. Some trim carpentry applications, such as installing crown molding, will require compound angles for the pieces to fit properly together. A

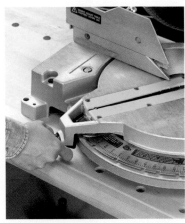

To cut miters on a power miter saw, set the blade at 90° and twist the saw base to set the cutting angle.

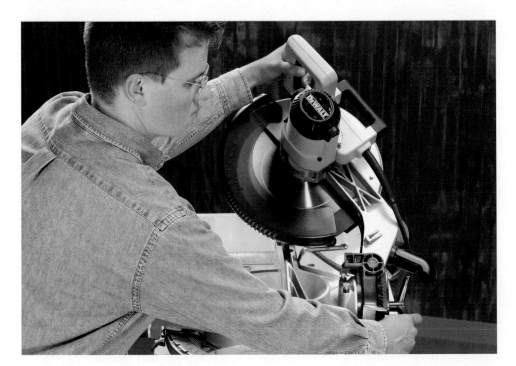

For bevel-cutting with a power miter saw, tilt the motor head and blade to establish the cutting angle. Keep the saw base set at 0°.

Bevel-cutting with a circular saw involves tipping the base off of 90° using the tool's bevel scale as a guide.

compound miter angle means the machine is swiveled left or right for the miter angle setting and also tipped to a certain bevel angle.

Cutting miters and bevels with a circular saw or jig saw: Making miter cuts with either of these tools is a matter of following an angled cutting line on the face of a workpiece. The same principles apply to miter cutting as crosscutting: For rough cuts, guide the tool freehand, cutting just outside your layout line, then clean up the sawn edge with a jointer, hand plane, or sander. For better control and cleaner cuts, run the saw base against a straightedge.

The bases of both circular saws and jig saws can be tipped to form bevel cuts. Given the small size of the bevel tilt scale on a jig saw, setting bevel angles with the scale is a "ballpark" determination at best. A more reliable method is to set the saw base angle off of a bevel gauge locked to the correct angle.

Cutting miters and bevels with a band saw: Cutting miters on a band saw can be done freehand, following a layout line, or by using a miter gauge and making the cut as you would on a table saw. Most band saw tables have a tilting feature for cutting bevels. Look for a protractor scale beneath the saw table with adjustment bolts to lock the table to different bevel-cutting angles. When bevel-cutting long edges, use the band saw's rip fence to guide the cut.

CUTTING CURVES

Three machines excel at curve-cutting. In terms of lowest to highest precision, they are the jig saw, band saw, and scroll saw. Band saws can only make curve

Setting up a jig saw for bevel cuts is easy using a bevel gauge to index the cutting angle. Tip and lock the base to this angle.

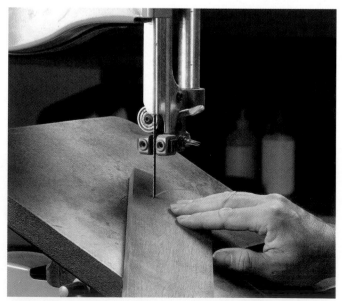

Tilt and lock the table on a band saw to make bevel cuts. Most saws have a protractor-style scale beneath the table for this purpose.

cuts that form outside edges of a shape because the blades are closed loops that can't be opened up to insert inside a workpiece. Jig saws and scroll saws can make internal cutouts as well as edge curves.

Cutting curves with a jig saw: The secret to cutting curves with a jig saw is to work slowly and not force the blade. Curve-cutting involves guiding the tool along a layout line or just outside of it using a moderate speed and the proper blade. Narrower blades allow the tool to cut tighter curves without binding and burning or breaking. Blades with larger teeth, especially those arranged in an aggressive offset pattern, cut curves more quickly than fine-tooth blades. For coarse, rapid cutting, use blades outfitted with 6 teeth per inch (tpi). Blades with 8 tpi are a good choice for general cutting and smoother edges. Use 10 to 14 tpi blades for the smoothest cutting. As tooth counts increase, cutting speed decreases.

Some jig saws have a scrolling feature that allows you to change the blade direction without turning the entire tool. This feature is most helpful when you need to saw into a confined space or when the surrounding material of the workpiece provides limited bearing surface for the saw. If your saw has both variable speed and a scrolling feature, it's often easier to make fine scrolling cuts with the tool operating at full speed. Feed the tool slowly so the teeth take smaller bites of wood.

Occasionally you'll need to remove the center of a workpiece without cutting from the edge inward. Jig saws make easy work of these sorts of internal cutout tasks. To start the cut, drill a hole inside the cutting area with a bit that has a larger diameter than the blade width. Use this starter hole to begin cutting out the waste.

Cutting curves with a band saw: Band saws provide more control for curve-cutting than jig saws, especially on smaller workpieces. The large saw table offers ample support, and the blade is held under tension so it resists flexing. You can also cut through much thicker stock with a band saw than a jig saw, and band saws can be outfitted with a larger range of blade widths and tooth counts to suit the task and cutting material.

Blades between ⅛ and ⅜ inch wide are the best choices for curve cutting. Narrower blades will follow tighter curves. Tooth counts will vary from about 12 tpi to 4 tpi in these width ranges. Tighten the blade carefully according to the tension settings outlined in your saw manual. Tighter curves are easier to navigate with a band saw by making relief cuts first, just as you would with a jig saw (see tip box, this page). When the design of the workpiece doesn't allow for

TIP: RELIEF CUTS

When cutting tight curves with any of the three curve-cutting saws, even narrow saw blades sometimes bind in the cut. If the blade binds or twists severely, it will break. An easy way to avoid this problem is to make a series of relief cuts through the surrounding waste material and up to the curved cutting line you plan to follow for the final cut. Arrange the relief cuts so they intersect the tightest areas of the curve. This way, you can break up a tight curve into smaller sections of waste rather than forming one long cut. You'll have more room to maneuver the blade through the curve without binding it as you proceed.

To cut accurate curves on a band saw, choose a narrow blade and guide the cut slowly. Keep your hands clear of the cutting path.

relief cuts, don't back the blade out of a long cut with the saw running. Usually the blade will bind in the process and pull out of the saw guides. It can even come completely off the saw's wheels. Instead, shut the saw off and back the workpiece carefully out of the cut.

Cutting curves with a scroll saw: No curve-cutting saw can compare with the precision of a scroll saw. The blades are incredibly thin and narrow for tracking curves with miniscule radii, and the machine cuts slowly so you can maintain full control of the workpiece. The basic procedure for using a scroll saw is the same as for band saws. Simply feed workpieces into the blade and move the workpiece right or left to follow the curve.

Scroll saw blades can be quickly removed and reinstalled for feeding into starter holes of internal cutouts. Be sure to orient the blade in its mounts so the teeth face downward toward the saw table. Tighten the blade tension knob until there's no side-to-side play when you wiggle the blade by hand. It takes some experience with the tool to determine just how tight to tension the blade. Overtightening will break the blade or cause it to pull free from its mounts. Undertightening allows the blade to wander as it cuts, causes it to cut roughly, and may cause it to break in a short time. If your saw has variable speed, experiment with different speed settings to find a speed that best suits the material you're cutting. Try not to back out of long cuts with the machine running. With the right tension and feed pressure, scroll saw blades can last for many cuts before eventually dulling or breaking.

ROUTING PROFILES

Woodworkers use routers primarily for shaping the ends and edges of workpieces into lots of different decorative profiles. However, routers are capable of performing several other beneficial woodworking tasks with the appropriate jigs and bits. They can mill rabbets, dadoes, and dovetails for creating joints. For

TIP: CHOKE UP ON THE BLADE

Whether you're cutting curves or straight lines with a band saw, position the upper blade guard and guides within ¼ inch of the top surface of the workpiece. This keeps the blade tracking properly in the blade guides, while it protects you from blade injuries.

Scroll saws are handy for cutting tight curves or making internal cutouts. The blades can be fed through a clearance hole inside a workpiece without starting the cut from an edge.

preparing parts, you can also use a router to trim workpieces to final size smoothly and accurately. Typically this operation happens by guiding a piloted flush-trim bit against a template mounted to the workpiece. Routers are even capable of cutting workpieces out of larger wood blanks or sheet material, but it's generally easier on your router bits to cut workpieces to rough size with a saw first, then clean them up with a router and template.

As edge-forming tools, routers are the next best things to dedicated shapers. Router bits come in a variety of shapes and sizes to cut such common profiles as roundovers, chamfers, ogee curves, and coves. Scores of other profiles are available, too. To cut profiles, you can guide the router over the workpiece freehand or move the workpiece over a router mounted in a router table. The freehand method works best when workpieces are larger than the router's baseplate and provide a stable surface for guiding the tool. In this setup, a fixed bushing or pilot bearing on the bit follows the edge of the workpiece during a cut and prevents the bit from burning the wood or cutting too deeply.

Using a router table for profiling is beneficial when workpieces are small. Router tables consist of a flat work table outfitted with an adjustable fence and mounted on a sturdy base or cabinet. The router hangs from a removable insert plate that fits into a recess in the work table.

Router tables make quick work of milling profiles on straight-edged workpieces. You'll feed the workpiece across the table and over the spinning bit rather than guide the router over the workpiece.

Freehand profiling: Routing profiles freehand is a relatively easy and safe procedure. Tighten the bit securely in the tool's collet, and clamp the workpiece to your bench. If all sides of the workpiece will be routed, set the wood on a non-slip rubber pad instead of clamping it down. You'll cut the profile by guiding the tool around the workpiece counterclockwise while pressing the bit's bearing or guide bushing against the edge.

Routing clean, smooth profiles depends to some degree on how you set up the cut and tool. It's important to adjust the bit depth correctly. Regardless of the type of wood you're routing, bits should not be set so deeply that they cut the full profile in the first pass. This overloads the motor, scorches the bit, and usually leaves burn marks or tearout in the wood. A better approach is to cut profiles in several passes, starting with the bit almost fully retracted in the router base, then increasing its depth with each pass until the full profile is formed. If your router has variable speed, adjust the motor speed to match the bit size you are using. Larger bits should be spun at lower rpms than smaller bits. To cut a profile, set the router base on the workpiece but keep the bit flutes away from the workpiece edge. Start the router and allow the motor to reach full speed. Hold the tool securely with both hands and feed it along the workpiece counterclockwise. Move the tool steadily and smoothly along the edge; stopping the router will leave a burn mark. Try to keep your feed rate as rapid as possible without lugging the motor. This will produce cleaner cuts than feeding slowly and allowing the bit to heat up the wood in any one spot.

After the first pass, readjust the bit for a deeper cut and make the next pass to mill more of the shape. If the little bolt that holds the bearing hits your benchtop before you've reached full cutting depth, slip blocking under the workpiece to provide more clear space. You may want to temporarily attach the blocking to the workpiece with hot-melt glue or double-sided tape to keep the two from shifting during the cut.

Profiling on a router table: Shaping edge profiles on a router table is a different operation than manipulating the tool freehand. In this configuration, you'll guide the workpiece past the bit instead of moving the tool over the wood. For routing profiles along flat edges or ends, use the router table fence as a bearing surface for the workpiece. Set the bit to full height above the worktable, but position the fence over the bit so just the first ¼ inch or so of the cutting flutes protrude past the fence faces. Be sure the bit can spin freely and does not make contact with the fence. Make the first pass, feeding the workpiece from right to left past the bit and against its rotation in a steady, smooth motion. Then shut

TIP:

When routing a single edge or end of a workpiece, clamp a pair of scraps adjacent to the corners of the workpiece where the cut will begin and end. Rout along these scraps as well as the workpiece. The scraps will keep the router from accidentally following around either corner and cutting into the wrong surfaces. The scraps also prevent the bit from chipping the exit end of the cut.

Start a profiling cut on a router table with the blade set lower than its full exposure. Feed the workpiece from right to left across the table and against the fence.

For large profiles, make additional passes raising the bit slightly with each pass until the full profile is formed on the workpiece.

off the router and adjust the fence to expose more bit for making the second pass. Continue to shift the fence and make more passes until the bit's pilot bearing is even with the fence faces. This position exposes the bit's full profile.

CAUTION: Feeding workpieces from left to right is unsafe for cutting the rough profile to shape. This feed direction, called "climb cutting," can allow the router bit to pull the workpiece with it as it spins, leading to loss of control of the workpiece. Some woodworkers advocate climb cutting for making the final smoothing pass of a profile cut. Use extreme care and hold the workpiece tightly if you try this technique.

Routing curved profiles on a router table: For routing curved edges, remove the fence and install a guide pin in the router table's insert plate to the right of the bit. It provides a bearing surface for starting the cut. Most manufactured insert plates are factory-drilled with holes for guide pins, and a pin usually comes with the insert plate. Without a guide pin, the only bearing surface for guiding the workpiece is the bit's pilot bearing. This setup is unsafe. You can easily overfeed the workpiece into the bit when starting the cut, and the bit will kick the workpiece back forcefully.

Without the router fence to limit the bit's cutting depth, control cutting depth by changing bit height, just like freehand routing. Set the bit low in the table to make the first pass. Do this by adjusting the router motor down in the router base.

CAUTION: Never adjust bit height by moving the bit up or down in the collet. If the bit is set too deeply in the collet, it will wedge in place and be difficult to remove. If too little bit shank is clamped in the collet, it can work loose and fly out of the machine.

Start the cut by holding the workpiece against the guide pin and moving the wood as necessary to follow the curve. Once the workpiece edge is against the bit's pilot bearing, you do not have to hold the workpiece against the guide pin. After making the first pass, adjust the router base to raise the bit height about

To mill a profile along the edge of a curved workpiece, remove the router table fence and install a guide pin near the bit area. Ease the workpiece slowly into the bit to start the cut with the workpiece pressed against the guide pin.

Guide pin

¼ inch and make the second pass. Continue raising the bit with each new pass until you've routed the profile you want.

Regardless of whether you are profiling flat or curved edges, keep your hands a safe distance away from the bit. Give your hands a space cushion of at least 6 or more inches from the bit at all times. Use push sticks or push pads to hold smaller workpieces securely.

Routing profiles along internal cutouts: You can rout profiles around the edges of a cutout inside a workpiece. For freehand routing, feed the router clockwise around the workpiece rather than counterclockwise. If you're using a router table, move the work clockwise around the bit. Always feed the tool or the wood against the rotation of the bit.

TEMPLATE ROUTING

Template routing allows you to use your router as a duplicating machine for making matching parts. The process involves guiding a straight bit along a shop-made template that matches the part shape you want to make. You can use a straight bit outfitted with a pilot bearing (called a flush trimming bit) to follow the template, or install guide bushings in the router base that fit around a standard unpiloted straight bit to rub against the template. Any diameter of piloted straight bit will work, but ¼- to ½-inch-diameter bits follow tighter curves and reach further into corners than larger diameter bits.

For profiling smaller workpieces with a router held free-hand, set the workpiece on a non-slip pad to keep it from shifting. Set the router for a shallow initial cut, and guide it carefully around the shape. Make successive passes at deeper bit settings until the bit cuts the full profile.

Tips for buying router bits

- **Buy carbide-tipped bits.**
  The cutting flutes of router bits are made of either high-speed steel or micrograin carbide. Carbide is significantly harder than steel. If you do only occasional light-duty routing, high-speed steel bits may be sufficient for your needs. They're inexpensive and resharpenable, but the cutting edges dull more quickly than carbide-tipped bits. For general-purpose or heavy routing applications, invest the extra money in quality carbide bits. They'll stay sharp much longer and cut cleaner profiles than steel cutters.

- **Choose edge-forming bits with pilot bearings.**
  Bits made for profiling purposes will have either a metal bushing or a pilot bearing for guiding the cut. Bearings last longer than bushings, and they don't spin with the bit, which leads to burn marks.

- **More flutes mean smoother cuts.**
  The more flutes a bit has, the less material each flute has to remove during a cut. Smaller cuts mean smoother edges. Bits with multiple flutes also offer greater anti-kickback protection than those with just one or two flutes.

- **When it comes to shank size, bigger is generally better.**
  Bits come in ¼- and ½-inch shank diameters. Some routers only accept ¼-inch shank bits, which is why bits of all shapes and sizes can be purchased with ¼-inch shanks. However, larger bits with ¼-inch shanks place more stress on the shank than on ½-inch shanks. If your router comes with a ½-inch col let, buy ½-inch shank bits whenever possible. Larger shanks absorb heat and stress during cutting more efficiently than smaller shanks. They also offer a stiffer spine to keep the bit from flexing or vibrating as it cuts. You'll spend a little more for the larger shank, but the payback is definitely longer life and smoother cutting.

- **Pointers for buying starter sets.**
  If you buy a multi-bit "starter" set of router bits, it should include a few straight and roundover bits of different sizes, a chamfering bit, and a Roman ogee bit. Some starter sets come with other profiles, but these four shapes offer greater general utility for the money. Buy a starter set to serve your needs for awhile, then add to your collection bit by bit as the need arises.
  Another workhorse bit to add to your collection is a rabbeting bit with interchangeable pilot bearings of various sizes. These usually don't come with starter bit sets, but they are worth the extra money, especially if you don't have a router table or dado blade for your table saw. One rabbet bit can mill an assortment of rabbet sizes simply by changing the size of the pilot bearing.

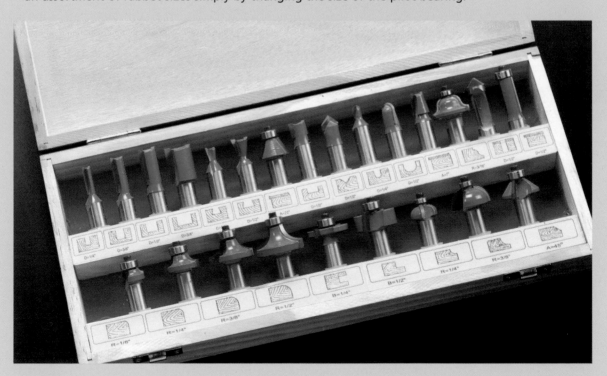

Flush-trim bit with top-mounted bearing: A good choice for template-routing with the router held freehand and the template mounted above the workpiece. The bearing rides against the template.

Straight bit mounted inside a guide bushing: This setup can be used as an alternative to top-mounted bearing. A guide bushing rides against the template instead of a bearing on the router bit.

Flush-trim bit with bottom-mounted bearing: Use this bit in a router table when the template is above the workpiece. The bearing rides against the template.

Successful template routing starts with a carefully made template. A template can be formed from any solid material or wood that's at least ¼ inch thick. Hardboard, plywood, MDF, or sheet acrylic are the usual choices. For template routing with a pilot bearing, cut the template to the exact shape you need and sand the edges carefully. If you'll be using guide bushings with the template, be sure to account for the offset between the bushing and the bit. To do this, make any internal cutout areas of the template slightly larger than necessary, and cut the outer edges of the template so it's slightly smaller than the final part size. You'll probably need to make a test template or two to find the exact template size that works for your guide bushing.

Use the template as a pattern for tracing the shape onto your workpiece. Rough out the shape with a jig saw or band saw, cutting about ¹⁄₁₆ to ⅛ inch outside your pattern lines. Mount the template to the workpiece, aligning the template with the layout lines. Use double-sided tape, hot-melt glue, or short brads or screws to attach the template to the workpiece.

Install a piloted flush-trim bit or unpiloted straight bit and guide bushing in the router. Set the bit height to a depth equal to both the workpiece thickness and the template material (for guide bushings) or so the pilot bearing on the bit will ride against the template. If you've trimmed the workpiece to within ⅛ inch of the template outlines, you should be able to mill away all the waste in a single pass. Start the router and ease the workpiece into the bit (for router table applications) or ease the bit into the workpiece (for freehand routing). Be sure the pilot bearing or bushing is touching the template, then follow the template to

Drill presses are handy for boring holes that are either perpendicular or at an angle to the workpiece. Tilting the drill press table changes the drilling angle.

trim the shape flush. Feed the work in the same directions you would for ordinary profiling. Work at an even feed rate to minimize burn marks and to keep the bit from tearing out the wood.

Once the routing process is complete, remove the template and clean up any sharp corners where the bit couldn't reach with a saw, file, or sandpaper.

Drilling holes

Sometimes your workpieces will require holes of various sizes or you'll need to drill clearance holes for driving dowels, screws, or nails. Hole-drilling for woodworking can be done with a drill press, corded drill, or cordless drill/driver. Drill presses afford you more control over drilling tasks than the other two drills, and they can handle larger bit diameters. However, you can still do clean, relatively accurate work with a hand drill if you don't have a drill press. Whichever tool you use, try to drill as carefully as you can, holding the tool so the bit meets the workpiece surface squarely. A quick way to check for square when using a hand-held drill is to hold the tool against the blade of a combination square with the head of the square resting on the workpiece.

For drilling holes freehand, mark the centerpoint of your hole, and tap a dimple into the wood at the reference mark with a scratch awl or nail. Set the tip of the bit in the dimple. Start drilling at slow speeds to score the entry hole and register the bit tip, then increase the tool speed to clear chips from the hole efficiently.

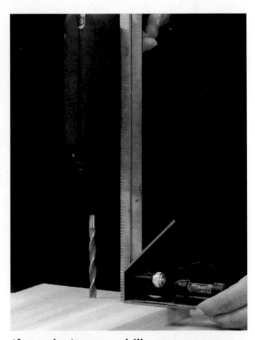

If you don't own a drill press, one way to improve your accuracy for drilling straight holes with a portable drill is to guide the tool with a square.

It's important to match the chuck speed with the size and type of bit you're using as well as the material you're drilling into. Changing the bit speed involves moving a belt to different pulley sheaves inside the machine.

Drilling holes with a drill press involves first setting the motor speed appropriately for the size and type of bit you're using as well as the material being drilled. Most drill press motor speeds are changed by unlocking and shifting the motor forward and moving a drive belt to different pulleys on two large clusters inside the machine. A few drill presses now have variable speed with a dial for adjusting chuck speeds. Check inside the pulley housing on top of the machine for a chart that indicates the right belt configuration to use for the speed you need. Larger bits require slower speed settings.

Counteract the spinning forces of a drill press by anchoring your workpiece against a fence clamped behind the drill press table.

Tighten bits securely in the drill press chuck. Use the hand lever to lower the quill—the vertical shaft that contains the chuck—and engage the bit in the workpiece. If you're drilling all the way through a workpiece, be sure the bit lines up with a hole in your drill press table (if your machine table has a center hole). Or place a piece of scrap material underneath the workpiece and use this as a backer when the bit passes through the workpiece. It helps minimize tearout on the back side of the workpiece as well as keeps the bit from drilling into the machine table.

When drilling holes larger than ½ inch, hold workpieces securely against a fence or scrap of wood clamped in place. Otherwise, the rotation of the chuck can pull a workpiece out of your hands and spin it forcefully around. With smaller bits, you can safely drill holes without the fence, but keep your hands and shirt sleeves well clear of the spinning chuck and bit.

Drill bits & drilling accessories for woodworking

Garden-variety twist bits drill holes through wood, but they leave a ragged edge around the entry hole. Several other bit options shown here produce cleaner edges and remove waste just as efficiently. Other drilling accessories cut larger holes, circles, plugs, and countersinks for recessing screwheads.

Brad-point bits (A) have a center spur for locating the exact centerpoint of a hole, and two sharpened spurs on the ends of the cutting flutes score a clean entry hole. Brad-point bits are designed exclusively for drilling wood. They come in sizes ranging from ⅛ inch to 1 inch in diameter.

Forstner bits (B) have a circle-shaped cutting head with sharpened rims or serrated edges for shearing clean entry holes. The center cutting area consists of a pair of chisel-shaped paddles that remove most of the waste in large chips. Forstner bits range in diameter from ¼ inch to 2 inches and are intended for use in a drill press. Use slower speeds when drilling with these bits, and withdraw the bit often from the hole to help clear the chips.

Spade bits (C) have flat cutting heads with a long center spur and sharpened edges on either side. Some spade bits have scribing spurs on the corners for making cleaner entry holes. Although spade bits are intended for drilling wood, they're better suited for rough carpentry jobs than fine woodworking applications.

Countersink/counterbore bits (D) feature a twist bit or tapered bit mounted to a counterbore collar. The collar has tapered cutting surfaces that enlarge the entry hole for recessing screw heads. Driving the bit so just the tapered cutters of the collar score the hole creates a countersink. Countersinks allow screws to be driven flush or slightly below the surface of a workpiece. By drilling the collar deeper into the wood, you can form a counterbore to recess a screwhead entirely below the surface, then conceal the screw with a wood plug.

Hole saws (E) have a steel cup machined around one edge with saw teeth, and the cup is mounted to a center mandrel that holds a twist drill bit. The twist bit centers the hole, and the cup saws a circular cutout. Hole saws are used more frequently in plumbing and carpentry applications than woodworking, but the range of cup sizes and relatively clean cutting capabilities make them handy for woodworking tasks as well. Hole saw diameters range in size from 1¼ inches up to more than 4 inches.

Circle-cutters (F) also drill large holes, but the mandrel holds an adjustable rod and chisel-shaped cutter rather than a saw tooth cup. To change the hole diameter, move the rod and cutter in or out from the mandrel. Circle cutters are designed for drill press use. At slow speeds and with a sharp cutter, they'll score holes with clean edges or create perfect wheel shapes from the cutout material. Toymakers use circle cutters to make wheels this way.

Plug cutters (G) form round wood plugs used to fill counterbore holes. They are typically sold in sets for drill press use, with each cutter sized to make a different diameter plug. Sharpened surfaces on the cutter score and remove material around the plug so the plug is formed inside the cutter opening. Once a cutter bores the plug, you remove the plug by breaking it out with a chisel or by sawing the board through its thickness to cut the plug free.

Countersinks (H) can be used in a handheld drill or drill press for scoring a conical depression around a drilled hole to recess screwheads. Countersinks with one or two cutting flutes cut smoother surfaces than those with flutes all around the cutter. The former are designed for wood and the latter for other materials, like soft metals and plastics, as well as wood.

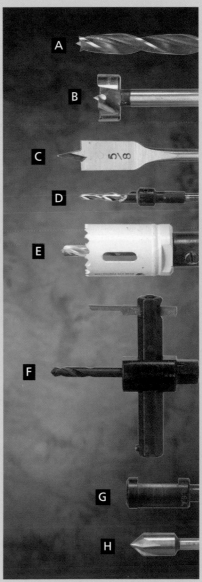

Chapter 5
PUTTING THE PIECES TOGETHER

Project assembly can be a gratifying, even exciting process, or it can be downright frustrating. Here's where a carefully designed, well-crafted collection of parts becomes that wonderful project you had in mind—or it's the stage in which you wish you had done a bit more planning, followed your drawings more carefully, or machined your parts with greater precision. Hopefully, a few setbacks here or there during assembly are outweighed by your successes. If the assembly process goes smoothly, great! In those instances where it doesn't, try to be patient. Many mistakes can be remedied with a little modification or by remaking a few workpieces. You might even discover a better way of building your project because a stumbling block crops up. Learn from your mistakes and take them in stride.

In this chapter you'll learn about milling joints, sanding, and installing common fasteners. Joinery might seem more appropriate for the previous chapter on making parts, but it really forms a bridge between part-making and assembly. We'll discuss joint-making here as an important step of the assembly process.

By the same token, sanding initially seems like a finishing step, not an assembly procedure. Of course, sanding involves preparing surfaces to receive finish. However, if you assemble certain parts before sanding them, they can be tough to sand carefully and thoroughly afterward. Try sanding into the back of a cabinet or the inside corners of a drawer box and you'll wish you had tackled this unpleasant job when the parts were still flat on your workbench and unassembled. There's no harm in sanding prior to assembly. Other times, such as when gluing up panels from narrower

COMMON WOODWORKING JOINTS

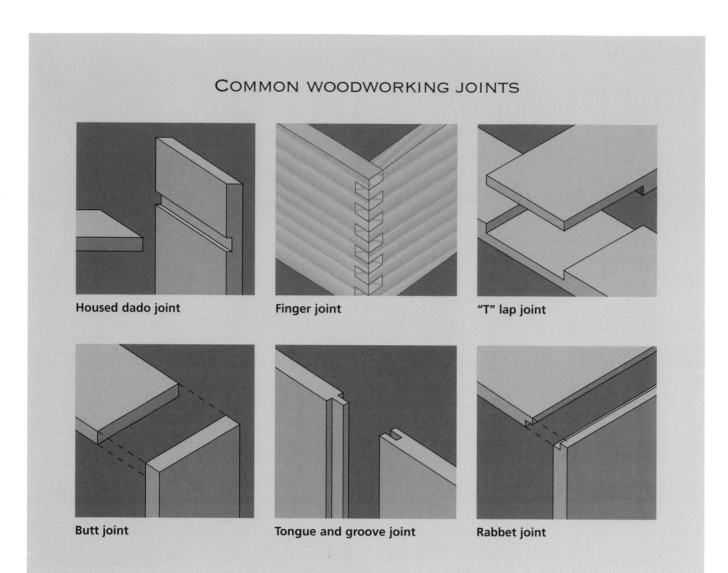

Housed dado joint

Finger joint

"T" lap joint

Butt joint

Tongue and groove joint

Rabbet joint

boards, there's no sense in sanding prior to glue up. These glue joints are easy to reach and must be cleaned up anyway after the clamps come off. You'll have to decide when sanding is more sensible or convenient—before assembly or afterward.

Making joints

Although today's glues and fasteners form reasonably strong wood connections between parts that aren't fashioned into precise joints, a bead of glue or a few nails often aren't enough to make joints that will hold up over time. When furniture or cabinet parts bear loads or brace against twisting, shearing, or pulling forces, they need to physically lock together. Here's where joints are important. By machining two parts so they interlock, friction helps hold the pieces together so the joint doesn't rely entirely on the glue's adhesive strength. When parts are intertwined, each part benefits from the grain strength of the other.

Another significant feature of joints is their pleasing shape. The classic dovetail or exposed finger joint, for instance, has those eye-catching geometries we associate with high craftsmanship. Their attractiveness disguises a more important purpose: All those pins and tails or fingers add up to huge surface areas for

BLADES AND BITS FOR JOINT-MAKING

Most woodworking joints can be made with a table saw, router, and a few different blades and bits. Whichever machine you use, the cuts you make are different than ordinary rip or crosscuts. For joinery, you typically only remove part of the thickness, edge, or end of a workpiece and leave the rest as a connection point for the other half of the joint. Since these cuts don't slice a board in two, they're called non-through cuts. You make them by nibbling away material with the saw blade or router bit.

When you cut joint parts with a table saw, a general-purpose blade will do the work accurately but slowly. For wide non-through cuts, a regular saw blade removes just a kerf width of material—only about ⅛ inch—with each cut. A more efficient option is to outfit your saw with a dado blade. Dado blades are essentially saw blades with adjustable cutting widths. There are two primary dado blade styles: stacked dado blades and wobble dadoes. Stacked dado blades consist of a pair of carbide-tooth saw blades that sandwich one or more chipper blades in between. The outer blades create the side walls of a cut, while the chippers shear away the rest of the waste. Chippers have only two to four carbide teeth, with each tooth mounted on its own wing of the blade. The chipper blades come packaged in a set with the outer blades and are manufactured in various thicknesses so you can "stack" them to produce cuts of different widths.

Wobble dadoes don't have chipper blades. Instead, a single saw blade is mounted on a large hub that holds the blade at a skewed angle. When the blade spins, the wobbling action removes all the waste material in the cut. The center hub is adjustable and marked for dialing the blade to different cutting widths. Twisting the hub changes the blade pitch and, in turn, the cutting width. Some wobble dadoes have two blades that form a "V" configuration on the hub. Adjusting the hub opens or closes the "V" and changes the cutting width.

Stacked dado sets have more components than wobble dadoes, and they're generally expensive. However, the higher price tag for a stacked dado blade is usually a good value since stacked dadoes make cleaner, more flat-bottomed cuts than do wobble dadoes. Whichever style you buy, select a dado that has a smaller diameter than the maximum blade size your saw can handle. For 10-inch table saws, buy an 8-inch-diameter dado blade. Larger dadoes are heavier and may exceed the capacity of your saw's motor and undercarriage.

The other option for cutting joints is to use a router, holding it freehand or with the router mounted upside down in a router table. Straight bits in sizes ranging from ¼ inch to ¾ inch will tackle nearly all the cutting work you'll need to do, especially if you own a router table. For router-cut dovetails, you'll need a dovetailing jig. Aside from straight bits and a dovetail bit or two, a piloted rabbeting bit is a helpful bit to own, especially if it comes with an assortment of interchangeable pilot bearings in different diameters. By switching the bearing, you can cut rabbets of different widths using the same bit.

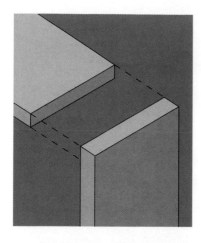

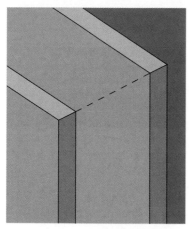

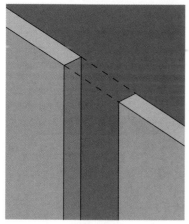

Butt joints take many forms, including end-to-face, face-to-face, and edge-to-edge combinations.

glue—much more area than flat edges and ends can give. More surface area improves a glue's adhesive strength. A thin layer of glue spread over a broad area is substantially stronger than a thick glob confined to a small area.

There are dozens of joint styles to choose from. To make your choices easier, we'll limit the options to a handful of different joint types, including butt, rabbet, dado and groove, mortise-and-tenon, finger and lap. You'll turn to these hallmark joints time and time again, whether you're building furniture or cabinetry. Even as your woodworking skills grow, this selection of joints will serve as the backbone for most projects.

Each of these joints can be made with different tools and sometimes in more than one way with the same tool. You can cut them with hand tools, but the process is easier and faster using power tools. We'll use a table saw, router, router table, and drill press here. As your skills grow, you might enjoy the challenge of making joints with chisels and hand saws instead of machines. Or explore more exotic and complex joints.

BUTT JOINTS

Butt joints are formed by pairing the ends, edges, or faces of boards and securing the parts with glue, fasteners, or a combination of the two. The mating surfaces of the joints are left flat, so butt joints can be quickly created. Butt joints that pair up long grain to long grain are the strongest style. Edge-glued panels and face-glued leg blanks are examples of long-grain joints. Both applications provide lots of surface area for the glue, and the configuration of parts combine long-grain surfaces with the grain direction going the same way. Glue alone will hold these joints together well.

When long grain is mated with end grain or short grain, the joint isn't as strong as long-grain to long-grain connections. End grain absorbs excessive glue, and short grain expands and contracts at a different rate. Either way, the glue's adhesive properties are compromised. Be sure to reinforce these joints with both glue and mechanical fasteners, like nails, screws, or dowels.

Making a butt joint: Since no special machining is required to make the two parts of a butt joint, the process is as easy as ripping or crosscutting the parts to size and attaching them. Much of the joint's strength relies on a good glue bond, so be sure your stock surfaces are flat and smooth before gluing and fastening them. If possible, joint or plane the parts smooth to remove any saw blade marks and optimize the part contact.

Spread glue evenly over both joint parts, assemble the pieces, and apply clamps (for more on clamping, see pages 114 to 119). When the joint dries, reinforce the connection with a few countersunk wood screws or finish nails. You can also drill holes through the joint and drive dowel pegs across the intersection of the parts. If you own a biscuit joiner, install #10 or #20 biscuits along the joint to make an all-wood connection with no fasteners showing. Adding biscuits or dowels strengthens the joint by increasing the glue surface area, and these fastening options can't back out or pull loose over time like screws and nails can.

RABBET JOINTS

Rabbets are two-sided cutouts that form a tongue along the edge or end of a board. The inside surface of the tongue is known as the cheek of the rabbet, while the flat area next to the base of the tongue is called the shoulder. Several different joints can be made by combining rabbets with one another or with other flat-edged workpieces, or by inserting them into a groove cut in the mating workpiece. When two workpieces are milled with matching rabbets and fitted together at right angles, the result is a double rabbet joint. By changing the size of the tongue, you cut a rabbet with a cheek wide enough to completely cover the flat end or edge of another workpiece and make an overlap rabbet joint. On ¾-inch material, make the tongue of an overlap rabbet ¼ inch thick and the cheek ¾ inch wide. Both overlap and double rabbet joint styles are often used for building the corners of boxes and cabinet carcasses. Overlap rabbets are especially useful because the rabbets hide the end grain of the mating part.

If you arrange a double rabbet joint so the boards are flat with the rabbets interlocking, the resulting joint is called a shiplap. Shiplaps are sometimes used to make large back panels on casework projects where the boards aren't glued together. The overlapping rabbet tongues keep the edges of the boards hidden even if they shrink. Shiplaps are also a good option for making wide, edge-glued panels because the rabbets contribute more surface area for glue than butt joints.

Making rabbets with a table saw: To make rabbets with a standard saw blade, cut the rabbet in two passes. Set up the first cut with the board standing vertically against the rip fence and on edge. This cut forms the rabbet cheek. Set and lock the fence so the distance from the fence to the closest face of the blade matches the shoulder width you want to make. Raise the blade until the depth of cut equals the length of the tongue. Make the first cut by sliding the board along the rip fence and through the blade.

To cut the shoulder and complete the rabbet, lay the workpiece face down with the unrabbeted edge against the rip fence. Reposition the fence so the blade will

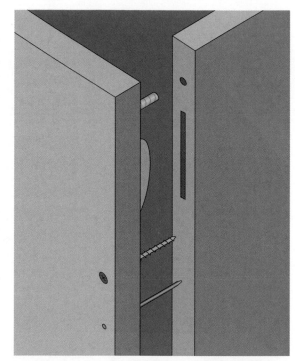

Although glue alone holds butt joints reasonably well, their strength improves dramatically if you install dowels, biscuits, screws or nails.

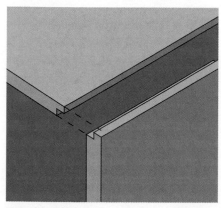

Double rabbet

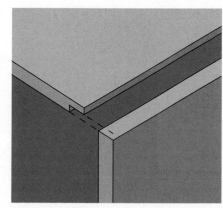

Overlap rabbet

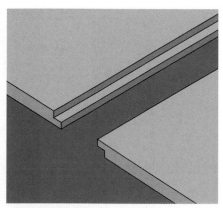

Shiplap rabbet

For rabbets that follow an edge, cut the rabbet cheek with the workpiece standing on edge against the rip fence.

Complete the rabbet with the workpiece face down on the saw table to make the shoulder cut. Be sure to adjust the blade height first, if necessary.

A dado blade partially buried in a sacrificial rip fence cuts rabbets in one pass. The blade trims the shoulder and cheek simultaneously.

meet the cheek cut when the workpiece is passed along the fence. Set the blade height so teeth intersect the blade kerf you made in the first cut. Make the shoulder cut by sliding the board along the rip fence.

You can make rabbets of any proportion using this two-step cutting method, provided the rabbets are on the long edges of the workpiece. If you need to cut a rabbet in the end of a board, it often isn't safe to stand the workpiece on-end against the rip fence. The longer and narrower the workpiece, the more difficult it will be to keep the board from tipping away from the fence or rocking back and forth.

A safer option for end rabbets is to use a dado blade and miter gauge. Set up the dado blade so its cutting width is slightly wider than the cheek length. Attach a sacrificial fence to the rip fence (see sidebar, page 95). Set the sacrificial fence so the dado blade is partially buried in it and the amount of blade exposure matches the cheek width. Raise the dado blade into the fence so the cutting height equals the shoulder width. Rest the board against the miter gauge with the gauge set square to the blade. The end of the board should touch the sacrificial rip fence. Make the cheek and shoulder cut in one pass by sliding the miter gauge and workpiece past the dado blade. Keep the board end pressed against the fence as you make the cut.

You can also cut rabbets along the edges of a workpiece in one pass. Set up the sacrificial fence and dado blade the same way. Run the workpiece edge along the rip fence like a rip cut and without using the miter gauge.

Making rabbets with a router: Routers cut rabbets accurately too, with the router held freehand or mounted in a router table. To rout rabbets freehand, install a piloted rabbeting bit and set the bit depth to match the width of the shoulder cut. Outfit the bit with a bearing that allows the bit to cut the cheek to length. Clamp the workpiece securely to your workbench with the edge to be routed facing up. You can also set the workpiece on a non-slip foam pad. If

SACRIFICIAL RIP FENCES

Oftentimes, joint-making involves setting the rip fence on a table saw close to or even touching the dado blade. This is a typical scenario for making rabbet or tenon cuts. Without modification, this blade setup is clearly unsafe and will damage both the blade and the rip fence surface. The remedy is to clamp or fasten a flat, smooth wood scrap to your rip fence. In this book, we'll call this simple jig a sacrificial rip fence. A piece of hardwood, plywood, or medium-density fiberboard makes a sturdy sacrificial rip fence. With the fence installed, you can raise the blade and cut a recess into the wood fence to provide clearance for the spinning blade. This way, you can set the blade so its exposure matches the dimensions you need for cutting the joint while having it partially buried in the sacrificial rip fence. The metal fence is safe from the blade this way, and you can set up the dado blade for a variety of width cuts without changing the arrangement of the chippers.

To make the initial recess cut into the sacrificial fence, lower the dado blade below the table, then start the saw and slowly raise the cutters into the sacrificial fence. Be sure the metal fence isn't crossing the cutting path of the blade before you crank up it up. Stop raising the blade when the blade height matches the cutting height you need. Never move the rip fence with the saw running, even after you've cut the initial blade recess.

your router has variable speed, adjust it for a medium speed setting and pass it along the board from left to right to cut the rabbet. Note: If the rabbet is limited to just one edge or end rather than extending around the board along an adjacent edge or end, clamp stop blocks to either end of the cut. These blocks limit the bit's cutting path to only the area you want to rout.

To mill rabbets on a router table, you can use either a straight bit or rabbeting bit to form the cheeks and shoulders. For straight bits, set the router table fence so the amount of bit projection out from the fence creates the cheek. Use the bit height to cut the shoulder width. Cut the rabbet with the workpiece face-down on the router table by passing the board from right to left across the table. Form the rabbet in several passes, raising the bit ⅛ inch with each pass until you reach the final shoulder width. Cutting a rabbet in multiple passes places less stress on the bit and produces a cleaner cut with minimal chipping and tearout. Press the workpiece firmly against the fence as you make the cut.

If you use a piloted rabbeting bit instead, choose a bearing for the bit that allows the bit to cut the cheek length, and align the router table fence evenly with the

front rim of the bearing. Cut the rabbet just as you would with a straight bit, starting the bit low and raising it with each pass until its height cuts the shoulder to width.

Assemble rabbet joints with glue. For joints that will be subjected to excessive loads or other stresses, drive finish nails, brads, or countersunk screws through both workpieces to reinforce the connection.

JOINTS WITH DADOES AND GROOVES

Dadoes are non-through cuts that cross the width of a board, in from the board ends. If you make the same non-through cut along the length of a board, following the long grain, the cut is called a groove. Grooves also refer to centered cuts made into the edges or ends of a workpiece. Both dadoes and grooves can be made with a standard blade, dado blade, or router and straight bit.

A piloted rabbet bit is the best cutter to use for creating rabbet joints with a router.

Dadoes and grooves can be combined with flat-edged or rabbeted workpieces to form numerous different joints. Among them are housed dadoes, blind dadoes, rabbet-and-dadoes, and tongue-and-groove joints. There are more dado and groove joints than are shown here, but these four examples serve a broad range of design applications and are sturdy and simple to make.

Making housed dado joints: A good way to strengthen a bookcase or cabinet with fixed shelving is to lock the shelves into the sides of the case with dadoes. The simplest way to do this is to leave the shelf ends flat and square and fit them into dadoes that match the shelf thickness. This way, the shelves are "housed" in the dadoes. One downside to this joint is the ends of the shelves show along the front edge of the bookcase or cabinet sides, but you can easily hide them behind a face frame, solid-wood edging, or veneer edge tape.

To build these joints, set up the width of the dado blade carefully. The dadoes should be a hair wider than the shelf thickness so the parts fit together easily, but not so wide as to leave a gap. Set the blade height for about one-third the

SAFETY NOTE: REMOVING GUARDS AND SPLITTERS FOR NON-THROUGH CUTS

Making non-through cuts with a table saw and dado blade requires you to remove the standard one-piece saw guard and splitter. Use extreme caution when cutting with an exposed blade. Make sure your blade is parallel to both the miter gauge slots and the rip fence. Tune up the saw if the blade isn't parallel. Guide workpieces with push sticks rather than your hands. Before making conventional rip and crosscuts again, reinstall the blade guard and splitter assembly.

thickness of the workpieces receiving the dadoes. Experiment on scraps to test the fit of the shelves in the dadoes before cutting dadoes across the actual workpieces. To make the dado cuts, guide your workpiece over the blade using the miter gauge as a backup. With the saw turned off, line up the blade carefully with your layout lines before beginning the cut. Always use the miter gauge to support workpieces that are narrower than they are long. Otherwise, the narrow board end tends to pivot away from the fence as you slide the workpiece along, which binds the dado blade and can lead to kickback. But if the dado runs across a workpiece that's wider than it is long, you can cut it without the miter gauge by guiding the workpiece end along the rip fence.

You can also cut housed dado joints using a large straight bit in a router. This router method is particularly effective on long, narrow workpieces that would be difficult or impossible to guide over a table saw. To cut them, first lay out your dado locations carefully with a long rule and pencil. Clamp a piece of wide,

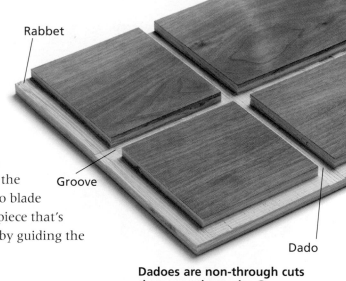

Rabbet

Groove

Dado

Dadoes are non-through cuts that cross the grain. Grooves follow the grain. Rabbets can follow or cross the grain, but they always occur along board ends and edges.

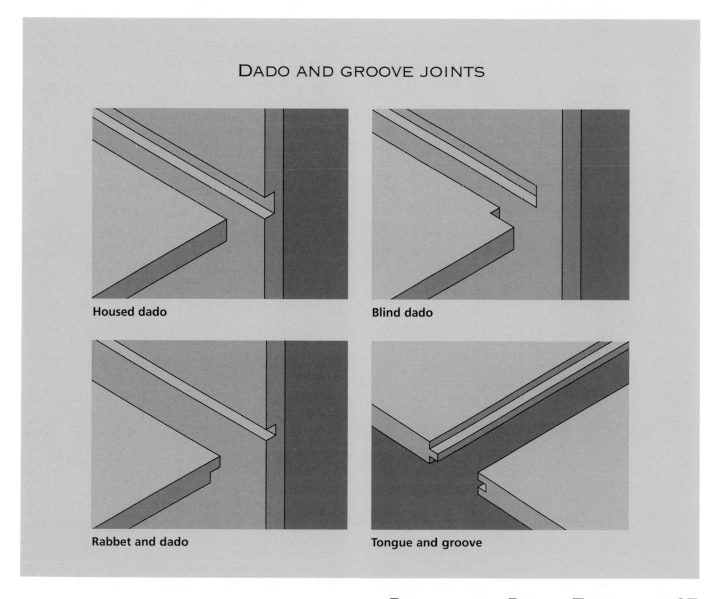

DADO AND GROOVE JOINTS

Housed dado

Blind dado

Rabbet and dado

Tongue and groove

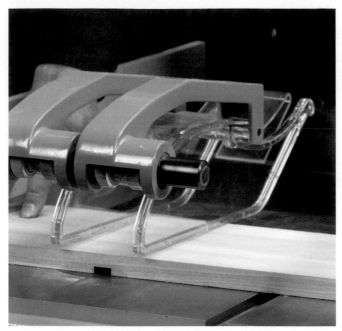

Housed dado joints can be cut with a dado blade on the table saw by guiding workpieces from behind with the miter gauge.

flat-edged scrap to the workpiece to guide the router along the cut. Install a straight bit in the router that matches the exact thickness of the shelving. Note: For ¾-inch plywood shelving, the material thickness is often slightly less than ¾ inch. These days, ¾-inch plywood is actually closer to ²³⁄₃₂-inch. Straight bits are sold specifically for cutting undersized plywood. Use an undersized plywood-cutting straight bit for a perfect fit.

Once the bit is installed, measure the distance from the cutting edges of the bit to the edge of the router base, and set the scrap straightedge this same distance away from your dado layout lines on the workpiece. Position the straightedge to the left or right of the layout lines. Set the router in place against the straightedge and check the orientation of the bit on your layout lines to be certain things line up. If you're cutting dadoes deeper than ¼ inch, make the dado cuts in two passes of increasing depth. This practice prevents overloading the router motor or stressing the bit. To make each dado cut, guide the router along the straightedge, pulling the tool through the workpiece toward you if the straightedge is left of the router. Push the router across the workpiece from front to back if the straightedge is clamped to the right of the cut.

Even though housed dado joints "capture" the shelving in the side panels, it's still a good idea to reinforce these joints with glue and drive finish nails into the shelves through the bottom of the dadoes. Long shelves can bow, and the deflection can pull the shelf ends out of the dadoes unless they are locked in place.

Making blind dado joints: For bookcases or cabinets without face frames, blind dadoes are a convenient way to hide the shelving joints along the edges. This joint still captures the shelving in full-width dadoes, like housed dadoes do, but the dadoes stop short of the front edges of the bookcase or cabinet sides, hiding the shelf ends. The front corners of each shelf are notched so the shelf can wrap around the stopped dadoes and still line up with the front edges of the side panels.

TIP:

If your outer blades and chippers form a too-tight fit for the shelving, no matter which combination of chippers you try, an easy way to get extra "wiggle room" is to insert a few paper or metal shims between the chipper blades. Usually, one or two shims will do the trick. This widens the dado blade just enough for the plywood to slide snugly into place.

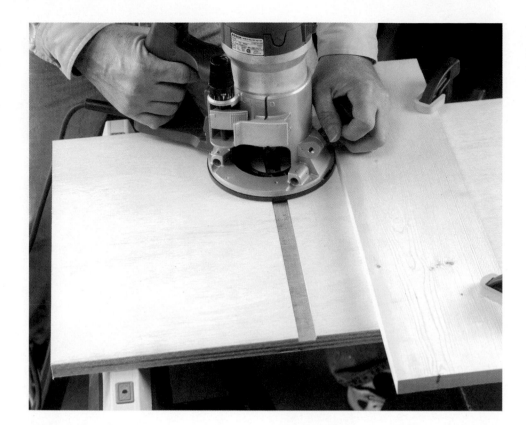

To cut a dado for a blind dado joint, run the router against a straightedge, pulling it toward you until the bit reaches the "blind" stopping point of the cut.

You can cut stopped dadoes on a table saw, but the setup is involved. If you're making a large bookcase or cabinet, sawing these stopped dadoes is also difficult to do accurately. It's easier to use a large straight bit in your router and guide the router against a clamped straightedge, just as you would for making housed dadoes. Lay out the dado cuts on your workpieces, and clearly mark the dadoes where the cuts must end to form the blind corner. Use the same offsetting procedure as described in the housed dado instructions to establish the position for clamping the straightedge guide in place. Set up the straightedge on the left side of the dado layout lines. Arrange the workpiece on the bench so the blind ends of the dado cuts are closest to you.

Cut each dado starting at the back "open" edge of the workpiece and pulling the router along the straightedge rather than pushing it. Slow down the cut when you are a few inches from the "blind" stopping point. Complete the cut by pulling the router more slowly along the straightedge, stopping the tool as soon as the bit reaches the end of your layout lines. Once all the dadoes are cut, square up the curved portion with a sharp chisel. Trim away the front corners of the shelving so the shelves fit fully in the dadoes and the front edges of all the parts line up.

Making rabbet-and-dado joints: When rabbets are paired with dadoes, the combination creates a strong, interlocking joint that has several woodworking applications. Rabbet-and-dadoes are often used like housed or blind dadoes to fit shelving into bookcase or cabinet side panels. The advantage of this joint over the housed dado is that you can use any conventional ⅜-inch straight bit in a router to mill the dadoes into the bookshelf or cabinet. No special undersized bit is required. The shelf ends receive the rabbets, which are typically cut

to fit the dadoes after the dadoes are milled. For ¾-inch material, make the rabbet tongues ⅜ inch thick and ¼ inch long.

Mill the dadoes by guiding your router and straight bit against a straightedge, or use a dado blade in the table saw and guide the workpieces with the miter gauge. These procedures are outlined in the housed dado joint description (see page 96). Cut the rabbets using the same methods as were described for making rabbets with a table saw or router and rabbeting bit (see page 96). Which tool option you use is really up to you. You can expedite the process by cutting half the joint—either the dado or the rabbet—with a router and the other half on the table saw.

It doesn't really matter which half of the joint you cut first, the rabbets or the dadoes. The more failsafe approach is to cut the dadoes first, then cut the rabbets to fit the dadoes. If you cut the rabbets first, it's harder to refine the shape of a dado accurately or easily. It's always a good idea to first make test cuts on scrap to inspect your router bit or saw settings before committing to the project workpieces.

When cutting the rabbet tongues, make them a hair shorter than ¼ inch so there's a bit of extra room in the bottom of the dado for excess glue to migrate. Drive short brads at an angle down through the shelves and into the bookcase or cabinet sides to lock the joint parts.

Making tongue-and-groove joints: Tongue-and-groove joints feature a centered tongue that fits into a matching groove on the edges or ends of the other joint part. Since the tongue has twice the number of cheeks and shoulders as a standard rabbet, it contributes more surface area to the joint for an even stronger glue bond. The interlocking nature of this joint makes it a good choice for assembling large panels for tabletops or for making back panels in cabinets and cupboards. It's also used on occasion to join the rails and stiles of small doors. In these instances, the grooves are cut along the full inside edges of all four door frame parts. This way the groove can hold a panel or pane of glass as well as connect the four frame parts.

Lay out the joints so the tongues are one-third the thickness of their workpieces. When the tongues and grooves are situated along the edges of boards, make the tongue lengths and widths match. Tongues measuring ¼ × ¼ inch are sufficiently strong on ¾-inch stock. If you are building cabinet doors, make the tongues on the ends of the door rails longer—½ inch is a good length for standard 1× lumber.

A dado blade will mill all the parts of these joints quickly and easily. Start by cutting the grooves. On ¾-inch material, set the dado blade for a ¼-inch cutting width and raise it to the appropriate height for your tongue length. Set the fence ¼ inch from the inside blade face for this operation. Guide workpieces along the rip fence when they are cut into a board edge. If you are cutting grooves into the end of a workpiece, first attach a tall auxiliary fence to your rip fence to provide additional support for long workpieces. Make the auxiliary fence 8 to 10 inches wide and attach it just as you would a sacrificial rip fence.

It isn't safe to groove the ends of a narrow workpiece without some form of backup support. A simple solution is to use a large piece of flat-edged scrap wood held against the rip fence behind the workpiece. Slide both the workpiece and the backup board along the rip fence to cut the groove. An even safer, more accurate method for cutting end grooves on long, narrow workpieces is to clamp the workpiece on-end in a tenoning jig that rides in the saw's miter slot. (For more on tenoning jigs, see page 107.)

When cutting the grooves, it's important that they are exactly centered on the workpiece edges or ends. You can form a centered groove by carefully setting the fence in relation to the blade, but there's an easier way to get the same result. Set the fence so the blade is close to centered on the workpiece, then pass it through the blade two times, flipping the workpiece from one face to the other after making the first pass. This way, even if the blade is slightly off-center on the first cut, the second pass will automatically center the groove. Be aware that this technique will create a slightly wider groove than if you make it in just one pass.

Once the groove is cut, make the tongue. The dado height you set for cutting the groove is nearly perfect for cutting the tongue to length, but lower the blade about ¹⁄₃₂ inch so the tongue won't bottom out in the groove. Install a sacrificial fence on the rip fence and slide the fence over until it just touches the blade. The blade should still move freely. In this position, the dado will cut a cheek and shoulder accu-

To cut the groove for a tongue-and-groove joint along the edge of a workpiece, set up the dado blade and fence so the blade is roughly centered on the workpiece thickness. Make two passes along the rip fence, flipping the board from one face to the other to center the groove exactly.

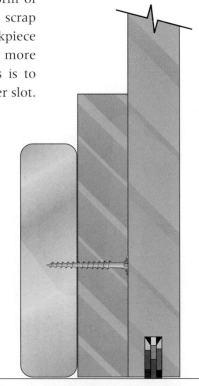

To cut a groove on the end of a long workpiece, guide it against a tall auxiliary rip fence and guide it from behind with a large piece of scrap. The extra support will keep it from rocking or tipping during the cut.

rately in one pass with the blade fully exposed. Cut one side of the tongue on a piece of test scrap, then flip the scrap to the other face and make a second pass to complete the tongue. Check the fit of the tongue and groove. The parts should slip together easily with just a slight bit of resistance.

Cut the tongue in two passes with a dado blade, flipping the workpiece end-for-end with each pass. Be sure to have a sacrificial fence installed for this operation to protect the rip fence and blade.

Tongue-and-groove joints can also be made on the router table. Here, a ¼-inch straight bit cuts the groove. Use a wider bit for milling the tongue, and make it in two passes, as you would if cutting with a dado blade.

Often, your test fit will require a bit of refinement. If the tongue is too thin, reposition the rip fence a hair closer to the dado blade and cut another tongue on more scrap. NOTE: *In this situation, you may have to lower the blade completely and cut a blade recess into the sacrificial fence (see page 96). Use the previous test scrap as a quick reference for resetting the blade height.* Correct overly thick tongues by moving the fence slightly further away from the blade to cut a wider shoulder. A single light tap on the fence might shift it just enough to perfect the fit.

If you'd rather use a router to cut tongue-and-groove joints, you can make both the tongue and the groove cuts on a router table. On 1× lumber, install a ¼-inch straight bit to establish the groove width, and set the router fence ¼ inch from the bit. Raise the bit so its height matches the groove depth you need. For ¼-inch-deep grooves, mill the groove in one pass, moving the workpiece across the router table from right to left. Keep the workpiece tight to the fence at all times. If you are cutting deeper grooves, make the first pass at ¼-inch cutting height, then repeat with more passes, raising the bit about ¼ inch each time until you reach the groove's full depth.

Switch to a wider straight bit for making the tongue. Set the router table fence over the bit, just as you would with a dado blade and sacrificial rip fence, so the portion of the bit that is exposed matches the cheek and shoulder dimensions you need. Set up the fence and bit to mill the cheek and shoulder with the workpiece facedown. Use a push stick to guide the workpiece and hold it securely against the fence and table. Push the workpiece across the router table from right to left. Flip the workpiece over and repeat the cut to form the second cheek and shoulder. Make these cuts on test scrap first to ensure the tongue you make will fit the groove. Lower the bit slightly to make wider tongues, or raise the bit to trim thinner tongues.

Another option for cutting the tongues is to use a piloted rabbeting bit and guide the router freehand over the workpiece. Follow the same procedure as you would for cutting rabbets with this bit. Select a bearing for the

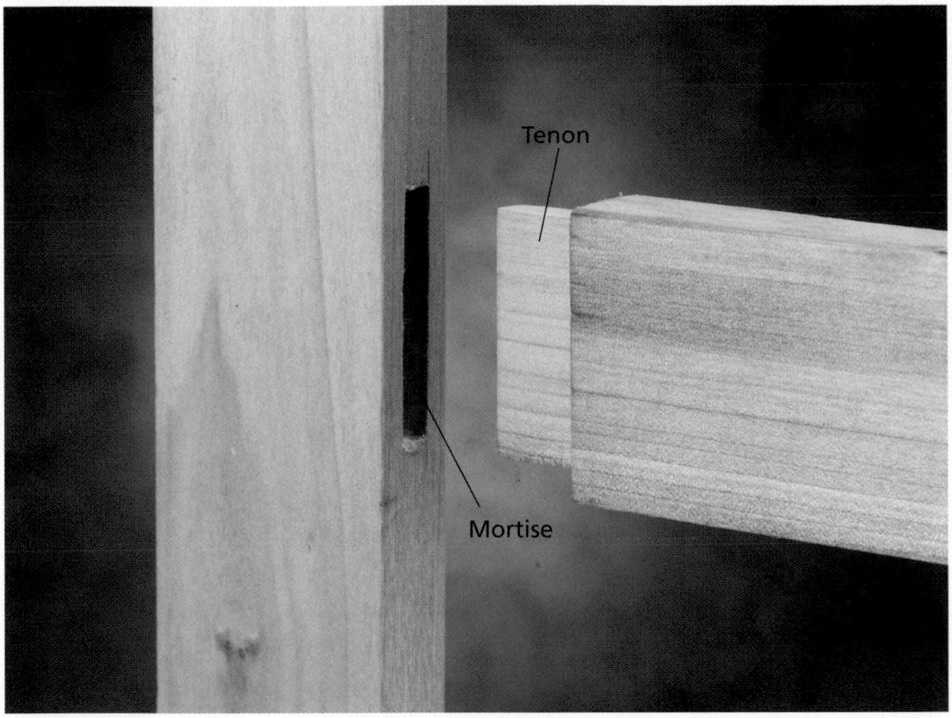

Tenon

Mortise

bit that will allow it to cut the proper cheek and shoulder sizes.

MORTISE-AND-TENON JOINTS

Mortise and tenons combine a four-shouldered tongue, called a *tenon*, with a stopped groove, called a *mortise*, to form an incredibly strong interlocking joint. Craftspeople have used them for centuries in situations where strength and stress resistance are paramount. You'll find mortise-and-tenons used most commonly to attach chair and table legs to aprons, rails, and stretchers. These critical connections are subjected to nearly all the different stresses that can be placed on two workpieces. There's ample surface area between the parts for a broad film of glue, and the joint parts lock together fully to add even more strength. Mortise-and-tenon joints are often pegged together with dowels or pins to form a mechanical connection, which will hold even if the glue bond doesn't.

As far as proportions go, tenons are usually one-third the thickness of the workpiece wide. Their length is determined mostly by the width of the mating workpiece that has the mortise. Some tenon styles stop halfway or less through the mortised workpiece, while other joint designs extend the tenon all the way through and even beyond the mortised workpiece. "Through" tenons are often wedged in place from the opposite end or across their width for greater strength.

The same names apply to the parts of a tenon as for rabbets and tongues. In fact, tenons are really just tongues with two more pairs of cheeks and shoulders on the short ends.

Making the mortise: The usual convention for cutting mortise-and-tenon joints is to mill the mortises first, then cut the tenons slightly larger than the mortises. This way, you can use a file or sharp hand plane to pare the tenons

One method for making mortises is to drill a series of side-by-side holes with a Forstner bit in the drill press. Back the workpiece up with a clamped straightedge.

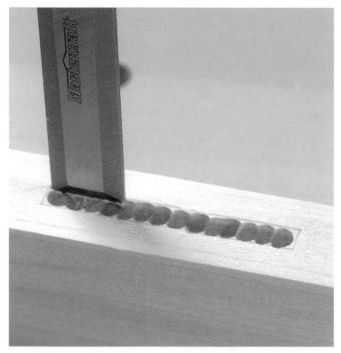

Pare off the remaining waste with a sharp chisel to flatten the walls of the mortise. Square up the ends with a narrower chisel.

down until they slide smoothly into the mortises. The rationale here is that it's easier to trim down an oversized tenon than shrink a mortise that's cut too large.

Mortises can be cut with routers and straight bits, chisels, dedicated mortising machines, or by using a drill press and Forstner bit. We'll use a drill press here. This method is easy to set up and control, and it yields accurate results without specialized equipment or jigs.

To drill the mortise, first carefully lay out the mortise shape on your workpiece. Install a sharp Forstner bit in the drill press chuck, and rest the workpiece on the drill press table to determine the drilling depth. Lower the chuck and slide the workpiece next to it until the cutting rim of the bit matches the mortise depth you need to cut. Most drill presses have a depth stop for drilling stopped holes like this cut. Set the depth stop so the chuck stops here. *NOTE: If you are cutting through mortises, with the bit passing all the way through the workpiece, slip a piece of scrap wood underneath the workpiece and set the depth stop so the bit will cut through the workpiece but stop partway into the scrap wood.*

With the drilling depth set, line up the mortise with the drill bit, checking to be sure the rim of the bit is centered between your mortise layout lines. You can line up the workpiece and drill bit anywhere along the mortise outline. Now clamp a straightedge or a fence, if your drill press has one, behind the workpiece without shifting the workpiece out of alignment with the bit. A straightedge prevents you from having to line up each hole you bore.

Set the drill press speed accordingly for the size Forstner bit you are using. A chart inside the drill press pulley cover should outline the speed setting you'll need to use. Start at each end of the mortise, drilling out the endmost waste. Bore the holes and withdraw the bit a few times to clear out the chips. Once the end holes are cut, drill more holes along the mortise, skipping a bit's width of space between each hole. The mortise should resemble a perforated line. Then drill out the remaining waste areas to open up the full rough mortise. What's left for waste amounts to little crescent-shapes along the mortise edges. Slice these away with a sharp chisel, guiding the flat back of the chisel blade down the mortise layout line. Tap the chisel with a hammer to make this clean-up work easier, but be sure to keep the chisel held vertically as you tap the blade down into the mortise. Cut the ends of the mortise square with a narrower chisel.

Making the tenon: Cutting tenons is similar to making a long tongue or rabbet. They're generally faster to cut on a table saw than using a router table and straight bit. Regardless of which tool you use, set up all the cuts so the rough tenon will be slightly thicker than the mortise you've just cut. If the tenon turns out too narrow, it will fit loosely in the mortise and compromise a significant amount of joint strength. Aim for making the rough tenon about 1/16 inch oversize.

Cutting tenons on a table saw is straightforward and simple to do with either a standard saw blade or a dado blade. Cheek and shoulder cuts can be made with a standard saw blade in two ways: First, you can cut the tenon cheeks and shoulders with the workpiece laying flat on the saw table and against the miter gauge. The process involves nibbling material off the workpiece, using the standard blade like a makeshift dado blade.

Dado blades make quick work of cutting tenons. Clamp a stop block to the rip fence ahead of the blade to index the first shoulder cuts, then make a series of side-by-side passes out to the end of the workpiece to cut the wide cheeks and shoulders. Back the workpiece up with the miter gauge.

To set up the cut for this method, first clamp a stop block to the rip fence in front of the infeed side of the blade. Position the block on the rip fence so the distance between the block and the front edge of the blade is wider than the workpiece. Set the workpiece facedown against the miter gauge, and line up the blade with the shoulder layout line on your workpiece. Hold the workpiece on the miter gauge at this setting, back up the miter gauge, and position the rip fence so the end of the workpiece touches the stop block. Lock the fence. This indexes the workpiece off the stop block for cutting the shoulders.

Form the cheek by making a series of side-by-side passes over the blade out to the end of the workpiece. Flip the workpiece over to cut the second shoulder and cheek. If the tenon has cheeks and shoulders on the board edges as well as the faces, stand the workpiece on edge against the miter gauge to cut the narrow cheeks. You may need to change the blade height for cutting these cheeks, but keep the rip fence where it is so you can index the shoulder cuts off the stop block.

A quicker method for cutting long cheeks is to stand the workpiece on end against a tenoning jig. Set the blade height so the teeth cut to the shoulder line, and be sure to account for the thickness of the blade when lining things up so it cuts on the waste side of the tenon layout line. Cut the narrow end cheeks with the workpiece face clamped against a tall auxiliary fence on the miter gauge.

A safe way to cut tenons in the ends of long workpieces is to clamp them in a tenoning jig. Raise the blade high to cut the cheeks, then trim the shoulders with the workpiece laying facedown and backed up with the miter gauge.

Once you've made all the cheek cuts, trim the shoulders using the miter gauge with the workpiece lying flat or on edge. Install a stop block on the rip fence to index these shoulder cuts. Be sure to reset the blade height carefully so you trim just to the saw kerfs you cut for the cheeks.

A dado blade will cut tenon cheeks and shoulders more efficiently than a standard blade because it removes

Cut the short cheeks and shoulders of a tenon with a dado blade in a series of side-by-side passes. Use a miter gauge outfitted with an auxiliary fence to support the workpiece from behind right up the cut. Clamp the workpiece to the miter fence to line up the shoulder cuts, or use a stop block clamped to the rip fence for this purpose (see top photo, p. 105).

more material with each pass. Use the same multiple-pass technique as you would with a single blade to cut tenons with the workpiece flat on the saw table. Index the shoulder cuts off a stop block clamped to the rip fence. Then remove the remaining waste in a series of additional passes working out to the end of the work-piece to form the cheeks. Stand the workpiece on edge to cut the short shoulders and cheeks.

If you'd rather use a router table, follow the same proce-dure for cutting the cheeks and shoulders as you would for cutting tongues in a tongue-and-groove joint. Use a wide straight bit in the router for this operation. Of course, you'll need to shift the fence further from the bit than you would for short tongues, but the fence position still establishes the shoulder cuts. Set up the cut so the workpiece is facedown on the router table, and support the cuts from behind with a miter gauge or wide scrap as a backup board. Mill the tenon starting from the board end, and make side-by-side passes, moving the work-piece closer and closer to the fence with each pass. When the board end meets the fence on the last pass, the bit should cut the shoulder.

To cut the short end cheeks and shoulders, stand the workpiece on edge and back up the cut with a thick scrap backup support.

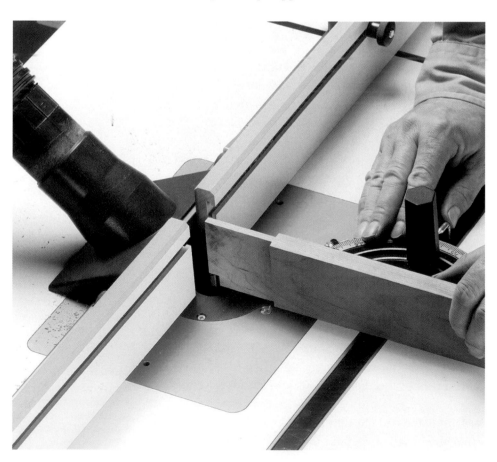

Tenons can be cut on the router table with a straight bit, if you don't have a dado blade. Use the router table fence to index the shoulder cuts.

Fitting the joint together: Once the mortise and tenon are cut to rough shape, try to slip them together. At this stage, they probably won't fit. Using a file, chisel, or sharp rabbeting plane, pare down the tenon faces and edges until the tenon slips with just a bit of friction into the mortise. Do this trimming work a little at a time, and check your progress frequently by test-fitting the parts. Once the tenon fits in the mortise, be sure the tenon shoulders make full contact with the mortised workpiece. If there's a gap here, trim a bit of material off the end of the tenon so it stops short of the mortise bottom. A little slip room here is helpful; it provides a well for extra glue to fill. Otherwise, the glue can actually hold open the joint if the parts fit too tightly.

When you arrive at a good fit, coat all surfaces of the tenon and mortise with a thin layer of wood glue. A paint brush makes a good glue applicator. Press the parts together and apply a clamp across the joint to hold it securely until the glue dries. To lock the joint permanently, drill a hole through the side of the mortised workpiece right through the tenon and into the opposite mortise wall. Drive a dowel peg into the hole, and pare off the excess with a sharp chisel or sand it flush with coarse sandpaper.

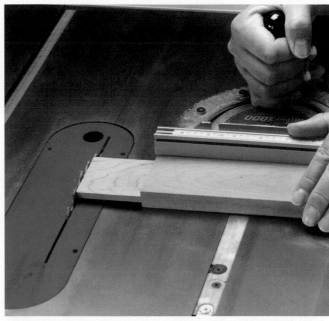

Once you've cut both parts of a mortise-and-tenon joint, assemble the joint to examine the fit. If the tenon shoulders don't seat against the mortise, trim a small amount off the end of the tenon to improve the fit.

TENONING JIGS

Cutting tenons with the workpiece standing on end is a balancing act unless you support the part firmly. It's difficult to move a narrow end over the blade without the workpiece shifting position either away from the fence or forward and back. You can buy a prefabricated tenoning jig from most woodworking supply catalogs that slides in your saw's miter slot on a metal bar. These heavy-duty jigs are typically made of cast iron, and they're outfitted with a back-up fence for supporting the work as well as a stout clamp for holding the part securely against the jig body. Most prefab tenoning jigs have a number of screw-type adjusters that allow you to move the workpiece laterally in relation to the blade, as well as tip it from side to side or front to back for cutting angled tenons. Expect to pay about $100 for a metal tenoning jig, which should pay for itself over a lifetime of hard use.

The interlocking fingers on a finger joint create a joint that is not only very strong, but attractive, too.

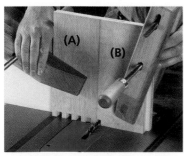

Once the first pin and slot are made, slip the slot over the jig pin and cut the second pin and slot. Repeat this process to cut the rest of the pins and slots across the workpiece.

The mating workpiece needs a slot along its edge so it will mesh with workpiece (A). Fit the first pin of the first workpiece between the blade and jig pin to fill this space, and butt the second workpiece (B) against the first. Make this cut, remove the first workpiece, and cut the remaining pins and slots in the second workpiece.

FINGER JOINTS

If you've ever run across an old wooden block cheese container at a flea market, you've probably noticed those attractive, interlocking square joints at the corners. Lots of jewelry box designs and tool chests have these joints, too. These wonderful, uniform collections of interlocking "fingers" and slots give the joint its common name, although it is also aptly called a box joint.

Finger joints are easy to make on a table saw with a simple jig that sets the finger and slot spacing. You can make these joints on your router table with a straight bit if your table is equipped with a miter slot. Follow the same construction techniques described below if you opt for the router table method, and use the same jig to cut the parts. Mill the slots between the fingers in single passes with a straight bit that has a diameter matching the finger widths you want to make.

For ¾-inch material, a good pin and slot width is ¼ or ½ inch. The best scenario for choosing a slot width is to select one that makes the pins and slots come out evenly across the joint. In other words, the joint looks better if the outermost fingers are full width rather than partial width. Use this joint when your workpieces measure up to even ¼- or ½-inch increments.

Making the finger joint jig: Build this joint starting with the jig. It consists of a wide, wooden fence attached to your table saw or router table miter gauge with a pin attached to the fence that matches the size of the joint slots. The pin is offset one finger width away from the dado blade or the router bit and serves as a spacer for creating the finger and slot pattern. We'll make the jig on the table saw with a dado blade. Clamp a flat, square piece of plywood or hardwood scrap measuring 6 to 8 inches wide by 12 to 18 inches long to your miter gauge fence. You'll be cutting the joint workpieces on end, so the fence must be tall enough to provide adequate support. Install a dado blade in the saw and set the width of cut to match the finger/slot width. Raise the blade so it will cut the full depth of the slots—they should be as deep as the mating workpiece is thick. On 1x stock, set the blade for ¾-inch cutting height.

With the jig fence clamped in place so it's roughly centered right to left on the miter gauge, cut one slot through the fence. Glue a hardwood pin into this slot so it projects about ¾ inch in front of the fence. The pin should fit the slot snugly before glue is applied. Then reset the fence on the miter gauge, sliding the pin exactly one finger width away from the dado blade, right or left. The spacing here is crucial. If you have a piece of extra hardwood pin stock, use this as a spacer between the pin on the jig and the dado blade to set the fence position. Screw the fence to the jig in this position, and try the following procedure on scrap before you cut your actual workpieces. If the joint parts don't fit properly when you finish cutting your scrap test pieces, the culprit is an inaccurate gap between the blade and jig pin. Reset the fence slightly to perfect the gap spacing, and make more test cuts.

Making the joint: Butt the first workpiece against the pin with the board standing on its end. Clamp or hold it firmly to the jig fence, and slide the jig through the blade to cut the first finger. Reposition the workpiece on the jig so the slot you've just cut straddles the jig pin, then cut the second finger and slot. Repeat this procedure to cut all the remaining fingers and slots across the work-piece. If the workpiece measures accurately to a width that's evenly divisible by the finger/slot width, the last slot or finger on the board end should be full size. When you're finished, flip the board end over end to cut a matching pattern of pins and slots on the other end.

Form the mating part of the joint: Fit the first slot you cut in the first work-piece over the jig pin so one pin on that board fills the gap between the blade and the jig. Butt the other workpiece against its mate. This way, the second board will receive a slot along the edge for the first cut and not form a finger here. Slide both workpieces through the blade to cut the initial slot, then remove the first workpiece. Slip the slot of the second workpiece over the jig pin, and make a second pass to cut its first finger. Repeat the slot-cutting technique across the board, then flip it end-over-end and use the first workpiece again to set the first slot cut.

When all the joints are cut, they should fit together snugly but without force or gaps between the slots and pins. If the fit is just slightly off, you may be able to fudge the fit by sanding the fingers and slots slightly. In cases where the misfit is too great to fit the parts together at all, adjust the jig on the miter fence and cut new workpieces. There's no other way to perfect the fit than to adjust the jig in relation to the blade.

For properly fitting workpieces, secure the joints by brushing glue between all the fingers and slots and sliding the parts together. Clamp the parts until they dry.

LAP JOINTS

Lap joints combine wide rabbets and dadoes together so the workpieces cross at full width and the faces of the mating parts are flush. Typically, lap joints are cut halfway through the thickness of their parts. They're also cut wide

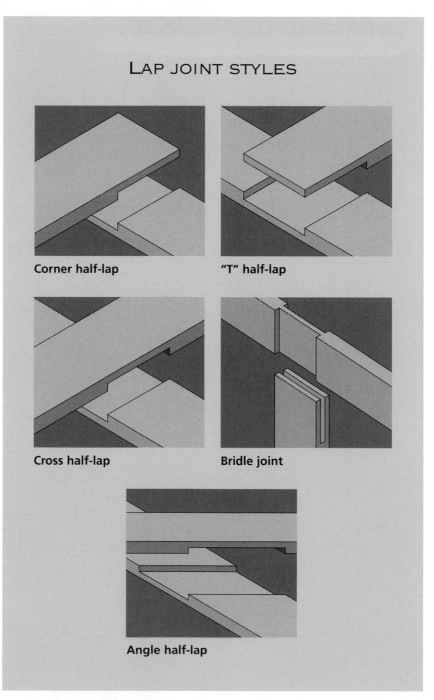

LAP JOINT STYLES

Corner half-lap

"T" half-lap

Cross half-lap

Bridle joint

Angle half-lap

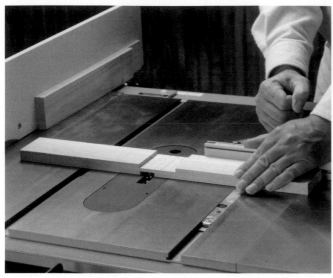

Lap joints are simply combinations of wide rabbets and grooves. Make them with a dado blade in a series of broader cuts. Support workpieces from behind, when necessary, with the miter gauge.

enough to house a rabbet tongue or a matching dado that's as wide as the mating workpiece. Lap joints may connect workpieces of equal or differing thicknesses, depending on the application, but same-sized parts are more common. When the workpiece thicknesses aren't the same, of course, only one pair of workpiece faces will be flush. Choose lap joints for building strong table and bench frameworks where legs meet stringers and aprons. The joints are interlocking and provide huge surface areas for glue.

Lap joints take many forms, as shown on the previous page. Corner half-laps combine two matching rabbets arranged at 90°. "T" half-laps couple an end rabbet on one workpiece with a dado on the other workpiece. Cross half-laps and angled half-laps form an intersection where two wide dadoes lock together at 90° or some other angle. Another, less common, lap joint hybrid is the bridle joint. Here, a pair of wide dadoes are milled into opposite faces of one workpiece. Make the depth of these dadoes equal to one-third the thickness of the workpiece. A deep end slot is cut into the mating workpiece to create two outboard tongues. The tongues fit into the dadoes.

There are no special cutting techniques for making lap joints, and the size of the parts makes these joints easiest to cut on the table saw with a dado blade. Set the dado blade for a wide cut to remove waste material more quickly, and mill the dadoes or trim the rabbet cheeks and shoulders in several side-by-side passes. For lap joints on workpieces with matching thicknesses, you can use the same blade height setting to machine both workpieces if you set the cutting height carefully. To help minimize tearout and provide more workpiece support, back up the dado cuts with a long, auxiliary miter fence.

Lap joints unavoidably form cross-grain connections. If the workpieces expand and contract significantly, the glue bonds will eventually fail. Reinforce the glue joint with dowels, screws, or bolts driven though both members. Mechanical fasteners not only strengthen the joint indefinitely, but they also add a bit of decoration.

Sanding basics

If your project surfaces remain fully accessible once you put the pieces together, you can skip the sanding until just before applying finish. But in many instances, such as building boxes, drawers, or chair and table framework, it's much easier to sand the parts prior to assembly. Sanding serves to level the wood surfaces so parts meet evenly. It removes dings, nicks, and swirls or minor burn marks left by saw blades and router bits. On a microscopic level, sanding provides "tooth" to the wood, so finishes have something to adhere to. But at its most basic level, sanding abrades wood surfaces so they feel smooth to the touch. Smoothness contributes to the warmth and completeness of a project done well. It invites admirers to touch and appreciate what you've worked so hard to make.

Dovetails

One hallmark of furniture quality for woodworkers and non-woodworkers alike is the dovetail joint. You've probably opened a drawer on a piece of furniture and looked at the corner joints just to see if the dovetails are there. We all do it. We all want to make them, too. Once you've made a drawer or other sort of box with dovetailed corners, you'll feel as though you've "arrived" as a woodworker.

However, venturing into the realm of dovetail joinery isn't easy. Cutting dovetails by hand with chisels and hand saws is a wonderful skill, but not one easily mastered by a beginner. It can be done, of course, but not without a good deal of trial and error as well as time. Your other option is to select a dovetailing jig that holds the boards in place and allows you to cut the angular pins and tails with a router and dovetailing bit. Machining them in this fashion is faster than cutting by hand, but only after the jig is set up precisely and you've made lots of cuts on test scrap. The close tolerances of the pins and tails demand that any jig be set within thousandths of an inch or the jig parts won't interlock evenly and easily. Workpiece widths and thicknesses also come into play and influence how joints fit together. If this doesn't sound delicate enough, the bit depth can also make or break how well the parts interlock. You'll need a router with micro-adjustment features to dial the bit depth slightly up or down. Suffice it to say, there isn't a fabricated jig on the market that takes the effort out of making dovetails.

If your heart is set on making dovetails, and you're a patient person, pursue them with vigor. All the effort will be worth it when your joint parts slide together satisfactorily and you bask in the well-deserved knowledge that you've made them yourself. Be sure to save your test parts and make notes about how you changed your bit or jig settings to arrive at a good fit. Your notes will be indispensable. Unless you make dovetails regularly, you'll probably need to put the jig away and remove the router bit to use the router for other tasks. Any way you can streamline your setup efforts will be advantageous the next time you need to cut dovetails.

Dovetailing jigs vary in the way they look and perform. There isn't a single industry-standard design. Consequently, describing the process here for cutting router dovetails would be limited to the design and method of one jig type. Instead, turn to magazine articles that review different jig styles to find a jig that the editors prefer, and read articles that cover a specific jig in depth. Or, talk with other seasoned woodworkers about the dovetail jig they use, then meet with them to try out their equipment. Some jigs only cut one style of dovetail, but those that make both both half-blind and through dovetails usually offer the better value. Jigs that allow you to vary the spacing of the pins and tails for making custom joint layouts are also beneficial.

Blind dovetail

Through dovetail

Sandpaper options and grits:
Sandpaper is nothing more than natural or synthetic grit applied to different kinds of heavy paper or cloth backing. The three principal grit types are garnet, aluminum oxide, and silicon carbide. All three come in a variety of different grit sizes, from fine to coarse, which influence how quickly and smoothly they cut wood. Garnet is a natural, brown-colored mineral applied to thinner paper backing. It tends to wear out more rapidly than the synthetic options, but is useful for hand-sanding situations. You won't find it in disk or belt form for power sanders because it tends to clog up quickly. Aluminum oxide is a synthetic material with tougher working characteristics than garnet. The particles fracture during use to expose new, sharp cutting edges. Aluminum oxide is applied to backing papers that are suitable for both hand- and power-sanding wood. Silicon carbide, the toughest grit type, is also a synthetic grit. Typically you'll find it on fine-grit sandpapers over 150-grit. Silicon carbide sandpaper is intended for wet sanding finishes between coats or to prepare metal for painting.

A variety of sanding products takes some of the chore out of sanding. In addition to conventional sandpaper, you can find sanding blocks, sponges, contour sanders, sanding cord, and sanding belts.

In addition to flat-sheet paper, there are a variety of other sanding tools made for hand-sanding use. Rubber or wood sanding blocks make it easy to hold sheet sandpaper and level a surface evenly. You'll also find foam sponges with sandpaper grit applied, for sanding irregular or contoured surfaces. Sanding grit even comes on a spool for cleaning up thin reveals and narrow routed details.

Choosing grits: Grit numbers refer to industry standards that regulate the size of the grit particles. As the number increases, the grit size gets smaller. Low numbers are for heavy stock removal, and high numbers are intended for finer smoothing.

For smoothing away imperfections on bare wood, 60-grit paper is the coarsest grit you should ever need to use. Start with this grit if your workpieces have deep scratches or burn marks left by sawing and routing. Once the large blemishes are sanded away, switch to 80-grit paper to remove the abrading left by the 60-grit paper. If your project parts are relatively smooth to begin with and you need to remove just light milling marks or scratches, start with 100-grit paper. Once you've smoothed away the noticeable imperfections, switch to 150- or 180-grit paper and sand again. As you move into progressively finer grits, you'll still leave scratches—that's how sandpaper does its job. But the scratch marks become so tiny that you can't see or feel them in the wood. Most experts agree that you can stop sanding after carefully working the surfaces with 180-grit or 220-grit paper. The scratches at this stage won't be noticeable under any wood finish. Continuing with even finer-grit papers can actually burnish the wood surface, which means the wood pores close up and inhibit the adhesion of the finish. Believe it or not, you can actually sand too much.

Sanding in four stages: Here's an easy four-step technique to follow for sanding by hand or with portable sanders. Follow this approach and your workpieces will be set for assembly or finishing, whichever stage you are at with your project. First, sand all the surfaces of a workpiece in one direction, moving the sandpaper at roughly 45° to the long grain. For reasonably smooth wood without major blemishes or scratches, use 100-grit paper for this angled sanding work. *NOTE: Always sand in the general direction of the grain. Sanding across the grain inevitably leads to scratches that are difficult to remove.* Sand in broad, overlapping strokes, keeping power sanders moving across the workpiece at all times. Once you've sanded the entire workpiece, switch to the opposite direction at 45° and sand the surfaces again with 100-grit paper to remove the scratches left in the first sanding stage. Next, remove the angled scratch marks by sanding with the grain using 100-grit paper. Switch to 150-grit and repeat all three steps. To ensure that all power sander scratches are removed, finish up with a light sanding by hand using 180- or 220-grit paper. Sand with the grain only on this last step. Note: For sanding the edges on 1× or thinner stock, sand lengthwise, with the grain. It isn't practical to sand these surfaces at opposing angles, and you'll likely bring the corners out of square by doing so. Go easy when you sand end grain. Deep scratches are harder to remove here.

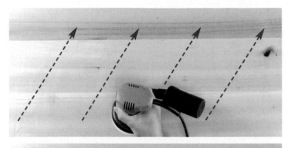

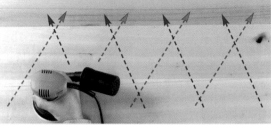

The four stages of sanding include: A) Sanding at a 45° angle to the grain; B) Sanding at the opposite 45° angle; C) Sanding with the grain to remove the crossgrain sanding scratches; and D) Removing the long-grain power-sanding scratches by hand sanding. Follow this four-step process for each grit, moving to progressively finer grits up to 180- or 220-grit.

TIP: CHECKING FOR SCRATCHES

If you think you're finished sanding a workpiece, one way to be sure is to dampen the surfaces by wiping with mineral spirits. Mineral spirits will highlight any scratches that should be attended to without raising the wood grain. Shine a light across your dampened workpiece. If you can see scratches now, they'll show up later under a stained or clear finish. Keep sanding, and wipe the surfaces again with mineral spirits to check your progress. It's worth the effort.

Gluing & clamping basics

Unless the parts of your project are moveable or designed to be disassembled for storage or transport, you'll generally glue them together permanently. Sometimes you can simply spread glue between two joint parts and secure the joint with nails, screws, or other mechanical fasteners while the glue is still wet. In most cases, you'll want to hold the parts immobile with clamps while the glue cures. Here's a general overview of the issues you'll need to consider when using glue and clamps.

Choosing a glue: Unless you are building regularly and using large amounts of glue, it's a good practice to buy only a reasonable amount of the glue you really need, use it as soon as possible, and then buy more glue from fresher stock. Some glues have a "shelf life" of only a year or two before thickening and losing their adhesive properties. Containers that hold from 8 ounces to a quart of glue are more than enough for assembling average to large projects. Leave the gallon-sized jugs for the pros.

If you buy only one type of wood glue for your projects, make it yellow wood glue. Technically called aliphatic resin glue, yellow wood glue will perform almost all wood-to-wood gluing situations exceptionally well, provided the surfaces are clean, flat, and smooth. It's the most common woodworking glue, available in formulations for both interior and exterior applications. Yellow wood glue cleans up with soapy water when it's still wet and spreads easily. It also has a moderately long "open time," which is the time you have to alter the connection or disassemble the parts before the glue sets and cures. You can even buy it blended with a dark pigment so it hides better under the finishes of darker-colored woods, such as walnut. Yellow glue is also non-toxic in both wet and cured forms. One downside to yellow glue is that it will not absorb stains or dyes, so be sure to remove all excess adhesive or the glue will show through the finish.

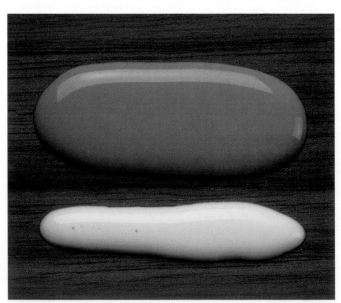

Aliphatic resin wood glue isn't just yellow anymore. For gluing up darker woods, like walnut, brown tinted glue blends in better.

Glue application and clean-up: For gluing edge and face joints, apply a bead of glue over each part surface and spread the glue out into a thin film that covers the full contact area. Use a paint or foam brush, a scrap of wood, or even your finger to do this. Aim for a thinner, rather than a thicker, film on both surfaces. Too much glue will simply squeeze out of the joint and be wasted when you apply clamps. Wet glue also acts as a lubricant between two parts. The more glue that's present, the more slippery the parts will be.

Press the parts together until the surfaces meet fully and the joint parts are flush. For gluing board edges or faces together where the parts meet but do not interlock, slide them back and forth to drive glue into the wood pores. Apply a few clamps across the joint where possible, and tighten the clamps just enough to close any small gaps that may be present between the parts. Over-tightening

The secret to a strong glue joint is to coat both mating surfaces with an even, thin layer of glue. Be sure the parts to be joined are smooth, flat and clean, first.

the clamps can break the wood, distort the joint, or force too much glue out of the joint and compromise the bond strength. If it seems to take too much clamping pressure to close a joint, the joint parts need more flattening with tools, or you may have trapped a bit of debris between the parts. Pull the parts open and inspect them. Clean off the glue, if necessary, and check the part fit again. Clamps are not a remedy for fixing misfitting parts.

When gluing up individual boards to make larger panels, install the clamps both above and below the panel in an alternating pattern. This way, the clamping pressure is distributed more evenly. Too much clamping pressure on one face will warp the wood.

One way to tell you have a well-glued and clamped joint is when it shows a thin line of glue or tiny glue beads along the seam between the joint parts. If the joint drips excessively, you've either applied the glue too heavily or the clamps are overly tight. Wait a few minutes until the excess glue moves out of the joint. Recheck the part alignment to ensure that the joint parts haven't slipped during clamping. After 15 to 30 minutes, scrape off the congealed glue with an old wood chisel or putty knife. Wipe up any remaining residue with a water-dampened rag, switching to a fresh area of the rag with each swipe. Once the glue dries, you'll have to remove any remaining squeeze-out or smears by sanding, chipping, or using a sharp paint scraper.

When gluing dowels into holes or tenons into mortises, be aware that glue has a hydraulic effect if it is compressed into a tight space. Its volume can only be

WHERE NOT TO APPLY GLUE

Glue bonds are beneficial for strengthening most wood joints, but not all of them. Limit the use of glue or avoid it altogether when the grain patterns of two workpieces cross. Two examples of this situation are where solid-wood tabletops meet the aprons that cross the tabletop width, and where wood panels fill the inside area of a wood-framed cabinet door. In both cases, long-grain parts (the aprons and top and bottom door rails) cross the grain direction of large panels (the tabletop and door panel).

Wood expands and contracts most across the wood grain. Long grain moves the least. If you apply glue all along these cross-grain joints, the wide tabletop or door panel is trapped by the end aprons or top and bottom door rails and cannot move freely with changes in humidity. Eventually, either the glue joint will break as the wood attempts to move, or the wood panel will split along the grain.

There are several ways to attach cross-grain joints that still allow for wood movement. One method is to glue short blocks of wood along the joint but not at the ends. Or, install short buttons of wood with a rabbeted tongue into long slots in the long-grain part. The buttons screw to the panel. As the panel expands and contracts, the button slides along the slot. A third alternative is to drive screws along the joint into slotted holes on the long-grain part. Orient these screw slots so they cross the grain of the wide panel—the same direction the panel will move. This way, the panel can slip past the screw shanks without restriction. Rock a drill from side to side to elongate these screw holes into slots. You can also nail or peg a cross-grain joint, but leave the last few inches of each end of the joint unfastened so the ends of the panel can move.

reduced so much. The glue will keep joints from closing if there isn't extra room inside the joint for the excess to escape. Drill your dowel holes and cut your mortises a bit deeper than necessary so the excess glue has room to pool, and apply the glue evenly but sparingly. Buy fluted or spiral-cut dowels or score the sides of smooth dowels by scraping them through the teeth of a pair of pliers. This way, the glue will have channels to flow back up to the surface and squeeze out.

Clamp options: There are a variety of different clamp styles for securing workpieces during assembly. For gluing up wide panels or closing joints on long parts, you'll want to own at least a half dozen long pipe or bar clamps. Both styles feature moveable clamp heads that fit onto either a steel bar or a length of black ¾-inch gas pipe. One clamp head slides along the bar or pipe for making coarse adjustments, while the other clamp head has a hand screw mechanism for final tightening. It is fixed on the end of the bar or pipe. Pipe clamps are particularly versatile, because you can install the clamp heads on pipes of any length. For general woodworking applications, buy the pipe in 3- or 4-foot sections with threaded ends. If you need longer clamps, connect two shorter pipes together with inexpensive threaded couplings.

For clamping workpieces less than 2 feet wide or long, have a selection of shorter bar clamps on hand. Most clamps of this sort have a fixed head on the end of the bar and a sliding head on the other. Some tighten up with a threaded shaft outfitted with a twist handle. Others have a squeeze grip to draw the adjustable head closer to the fixed head. The squeeze-grip style bar clamps have a quick-release lever that loosens the clamp. Bar clamps have a series of spring-loaded slip plates that serve the same quick-release function.

C-clamps in the 4- to 6-inch size range are great for clamping small parts or holding jigs in place on

Wood clamps come in all shapes and sizes, from large bar and pipe clamps intended for clamping panels and casework to smaller C-clamps, wood screws, and spring clamps for smaller frame and part assembly or machining clamp aids. Even packaging tape can provide clamping pressure when needed.

TIP: USING PADS AND CAULS

Clamps exert tremendous pressure on workpieces, so much so that the clamp contact surfaces can easily dent softer woods. If your clamps lack protective pads, be sure to slip scraps of soft wood between the clamp heads and the workpieces before tightening the clamps. Sections of hardboard or even adhesive felt tabs for furniture work well for this purpose.

When gluing up wide panels using several narrower boards, oftentimes one or more of the boards will slip out of alignment as you tighten the clamps. One way to keep the board faces aligned is to squeeze them between pairs of cauls clamped above and below the panel. Cauls can be made from strips of any stiff, flat scrap material. Plywood or hardwood pieces 2 to 3 inches wide make great clamp cauls. A pair of cauls installed over each end of a panel is usually sufficient to keep the panel flat. Use short bar clamps to hold the cauls in place and long pipe or bar clamps to pull the panel together widthwise. Cover the edges of the cauls with painter's tape to keep them from sticking to glue.

router tables and table saws. Inexpensive metal or plastic spring clamps are also handy to have for low-strength clamping situations. Buy the type with pivoting plastic jaws or rubber-lined jaws. Wood screws, which operate by turning two threaded shafts in opposite directions, are not only helpful for closing joints but also do double duty as makeshift vises for holding parts vertically or horizontally during tooling operations.

Band clamps are helpful for securing the staves of round cylinders or holding odd-shaped assemblies together, such as chair legs and rails. These clamps have an adjustable nylon strap that cinches up with a ratcheting mechanism. In a pinch, a length of surgical tubing, a piece of rope, or even strips of packing or duct tape can become band clamps.

Corner clamps are handy for securing two mitered parts together. Picture framers swear by them. Each joint part clamps separately, and the clamp body holds the parts squarely until the glue dries or while you install fasteners across the joint.

Dry-fitting & staging

Before slathering glue onto your carefully crafted and sanded workpieces and clamping them together, plan how you want the assembly process to go. Think about the process of gluing and clamping like an exercise in woodworking surgery. In order for parts to go together as you hope, you must work methodically and neatly, but not slowly. Once the glue is spread, you'll have a limited time to assemble and clamp things together before the glue starts to set.

One way to prevent gluing and clamping headaches is to dry-fit the parts ahead of time. Be sure all the joints fit together easily without glue. If you have to reach for a mallet to pound things closed now, you'll probably have to do it again when you apply glue. Fix those tight joints before opening the glue bottle. As you slip the parts together dry, plan the order in

Before opening the glue bottle to begin a glue-up, dry-fit all parts of the project and install clamps to rehearse the best sequence for assembly.

which you'll assemble them. Stage some glue-ups ahead of others, even if it means turning one gluing operation into a two-day affair. Better to allow some stages of the glue-up to dry than try to do too much gluing at once. Write the gluing order down if need be, then follow it carefully. Sometimes it helps to label your parts, especially if several workpieces look alike but don't assemble interchangeably. If one piece must mate with another piece, mark them so there's no confusion.

Rehearsing your gluing and clamping procedure and dry-fitting the pieces is a good opportunity to arrange all the hardware and supplies you'll want to have close at hand. Install the clamps on the dry-assembled parts to make sure they'll work properly, then open the clamps a bit wider than necessary when you remove them. Lay them within arm's reach of where they'll be installed. Have a bucket of warm, soapy water and a sponge close by for wiping up squeeze-out and drips as well as to keep your hands clean while you work. Be sure there are shop towels or paper towels nearby, too. Line your benchtop with waxed paper, sheet plastic, or plastic trash bags if it isn't topcoated with varnish, to keep glued parts from sticking to it. If your benchtop is small and you have many parts to glue up, spread out some parts and supplies on another table to reduce the clutter so you'll have ample room to work.

Installing nails & screws

Once your project has passed through the gluing and clamping stage of assembly, you may need to reinforce the joints with additional mechanical fasteners, such as nails and screws. Unless you are gluing edges to edges or faces to faces, all other butt joints should be reinforced with nails or screws. Rabbet and dado joints also benefit from a few nails or screws driven across the parts.

Finish nails and brads come in a range of sizes. Keep an assortment of sizes on hand for general project assembly.

Types of nails for woodworking: There are lots of different nail styles, but for woodworking, finish nails are the best choice. The nail heads are small and easy to conceal with wood putty, and their slender shanks penetrate wood grain easily without splitting it. You'll find finish nails sold in a range of lengths and shaft thicknesses. The nails are sized by the pennyweight system, which pairs a number with the letter "d." The number refers to the nail length and gauge, while the "d" means penny. Pennyweight sizes start at 2d (1 inch) and go up from there. Keep a range of finish nail sizes on hand for all your fastening needs. You'll find that 3d (1¼-inch) up to 8d (2½-inch) sizes are most useful for fastening common 1× and 2× material.

For tacking thin or fragile workpieces together, use brad nails or wire nails instead of finish nails. Either option comes in lengths shorter than 1 inch, and the shanks are much thinner than 2d finish nails. Use a small tack hammer to drive these tiny nails. Hold them in place with a needle-nosed pliers to start nailing, and tap them gently to keep from bending or jarring them off course.

Installing finish nails: Use a medium-weight claw hammer with a smooth face for driving finish nails. On softwoods such as cedar and pine, you can often hammer them in without drilling pilot holes first. For hardwoods, don't skip the

You can conceal recessed nail-heads with tinted wood filler or putty before applying finish. Press it into the nailhead divots with a putty knife and remove the excess.

pilot hole. Drill the hole with a twist bit that's slightly smaller than the nail shank thickness to give the nail a good friction fit in the wood.

Once you've driven the nail and the head is flush with the wood surface, tap the head below the surface with a nailset to conceal it. Nailsets are made with tips of different sizes and are sold in sets or individually. With the nail head recessed, fill the divot with matching wood putty or wax-based putty stick to hide it. Note: If you are staining the project, wait until after the stain is applied, then use putty that's tinted to approximately the same stain color to hide the fastener head.

Common screws for woodworking: Several screw styles can be used almost interchangeably for general woodworking. Wallboard screws and deck screws have become widely popular woodworking screws as well as construction fasteners. Both styles have coarse threads that bite quickly into wood. Wallboard screws should be used only for interior woodworking projects, because they have no weather-resistant surface finish. Deck screws can be used for interior or exterior projects. Their galvanized or plasticized coatings stand up well to the elements, but they also can be hidden beneath putty or wood plugs like wallboard screws. You can also find deck screws made of stainless steel, which is impervious to corrosion. Drywall and deck screws are sold by length, not by gauge. Keep a supply of sizes ranging from 1¼ inches to 3 inches in your shop.

In the fine woodworking arena, most professionals choose flathead wood screws over construction screws. Wood screws have thicker shanks and finer threads, and the top portion of the shank has no threads. The bare shank prevents the top half of the joint from lifting away from the bottom half as the screw is driven home.

Wood screws are made of several metals, including bright or brass-coated steel, solid brass, and stainless. They're sized by gauges ranging from 0 to 12. Both the shank thickness and the screw length increase as the number of the gauge goes up. You'll find wood screws sold by both gauge and length. For most uses, #6- to #10-gauge wood screws will serve your needs. Choose Phillips-style or square-drive screw head patterns over slotted styles made for flat-blade screwdrivers. Flat-blade screws are harder to drive without stripping the head or marring your work with the screwdriver tip.

Installing screws: You'll never regret drilling pilot holes for any type of screw you drive into a woodworking project. Pilot holes prevent splits, even if the holes aren't necessary. If you are using self-tapping screws, you can skip the pilot hole. Always drill pilot holes before driving flathead wood screws or when installing any screw style into hardwood. Pilot holes are wise precautions for softwoods, too.

To drill a pilot hole, use a countersink bit that has a slightly smaller diameter than the screw you are installing. Make sure the overall length of the countersink portion and the bit does not exceed the screw length—slightly shorter is even better. Drill the pilot hole until the countersink portion of the bit engages the wood. If you want the screw head to stop flush or slightly below the wood surface, drill a little deeper until the countersink makes a tapered recess for the screw head. You can also continue drilling until the countersink flutes are buried ¼ inch or so into the wood, then cover the screw head with putty, or cap it with glue and a short dowel or wood plug.

If you use a cordless drill/driver to drive screws, set the drill's clutch for drill-only mode so it won't disengage under excessive torque. Stop driving the screw as soon as the screw head seats, to prevent snapping the screw. For soft brass screws, drive a steel screw of the same size into the pilot hole first, then back it out and replace with the brass screw. Use a lower torque setting on the drill to keep it from over-driving and breaking the screw.

When drilling into softwoods, you'll seldom need to lubricate the screw to drive it home. On hardwoods, rub the tip of the screw threads with beeswax or paste furniture wax first to make the screw easier to drive. If any wax ends up at the surface of the screw hole, remove it with mineral spirits before applying finish. Otherwise, the finish won't stick.

A good way to hide recessed screwheads is to drill counterbored holes and cap them with wood plugs. Use plugs of the same wood species as the project for best results.

Chapter 6
ADDING A FINISH

Most bare wood needs a barrier against the environment to protect it, enhance its beauty, and keep it looking great for years to come. There are many different wood finishes available, with a range of performance characteristics and application requirements. A few finishes are better left to professionals with specialized equipment and skills. However, finishing doesn't have to be difficult. You don't need be a chemist or a finishing expert to apply most finishes successfully. Basically, simple finishing involves three steps: First, you'll need to do some final prep work to prepare the wood surfaces for finish. You can color the wood if you wish with stains, then seal it beneath a transparent topcoat. Or paint your project instead. In this final chapter you'll learn how to apply several easy finishes.

Why apply a finish?

If you appreciate the natural look, smell, and feel of unfinished wood, you might wonder why you should apply a finish at all. There are a number of important reasons.

Finishes protect and seal wood from water. Remember that wood absorbs and releases moisture constantly, whether it is kiln-dried or air-dried, finished or unfinished. A topcoat of varnish, shellac, paint, or other finishing material slows down the rate of moisture exchange between the atmosphere and the wood, which has a stabilizing effect on the wood. Joints stay tighter, warpage is minimized, and glue bonds last longer. Topcoats also help seal wood pores against stains that develop from ordinary surface spills, dirt, and grime. The surface coating provides added protection from scratches and scuffs. Some finishes even have UV-protective additives to help slow the bleaching and damaging effects of sunlight.

Notice in these two oak samples how an oil finish leaves a matte finish with the wood pores open, while the varnished finish creates a smoother film on the surface that hides the wood's texture.

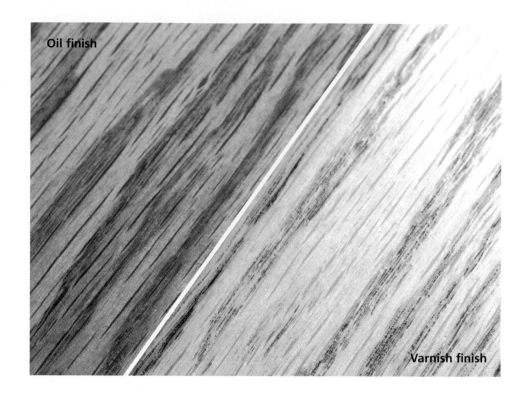

Oil finish

Varnish finish

Finishes also add a dimension of color to wood. A multitude of stain colors allow you to turn wood nearly any color of the rainbow. With tinting, less expensive woods can sometimes mimic the color of more expensive species. Hard maple coated with black dye looks convincingly like ebony. Red alder with mahogany-colored stain is hard to distinguish from real Honduras mahogany.

Aside from changing or enhancing color, wood finish allows you to modify the surface appearance and texture of wood. A wiping finish leaves wood pores largely open so you can see and feel the wood's natural surface. On the other end of the spectrum, a gloss polyurethane varnish imparts a slippery sheen for a "wet" look, if that's what you prefer. It fills pores and grain, levelling the wood surface. Open-pored finishes offer significantly less protection, but they are easier to apply. Varnish produces a film that is much more protective and durable, but it takes more time to apply.

Preparing surfaces for finishing

Thorough sanding is the best way to ensure that finished surfaces feel smooth and the topcoat layers apply evenly. Read more about how to sand on pages 110 to 113. A few other tasks also fall under the heading of surface preparation. Before coloring the wood or applying a topcoat, clean up any excess glue on the wood surface, and fill dents, holes, and other imperfections. If you're going to use a water-based dye, stain, or varnish, you'll want to raise the grain before finishing and sand again lightly.

A walnut stain on white oak (top) offers a darker color than a clear finish on actual walnut.

After you are finished with your final sanding, thoroughly clean off all sandpaper residue and dust by vacuuming the wood or blowing off the surfaces with compressed air. Either of these methods is more effective than brushing off the wood or wiping it with a rag. It is imperative to remove all loose surface debris to ensure that stain and finish will go on smoothly and bond securely to the wood.

Cleaning up dried glue: Even if you apply glue to your project with a surgeon's care, eventually you're going to end up with a little extra squeezing out here or there around joints. Even the smallest amount of extra glue will show up under a colored or clear finish like a traffic light, so it's important to remove all traces of dried glue before proceeding with stains and topcoats. Wipe your project down with mineral spirits, just as you would to check for surface scratches (see page 113), and the dried glue will show up as discolored areas on the wood. It's a good idea to do this clean-up in stages, wiping down and removing glue on one part of the project before moving on to the next. That way you won't miss any spots.

Dried glue won't absorb transparent colored finishes like stain or dye, and it will show up under them. Remove all traces of dried glue before finishing.

The obvious method for removing dried glue is to scrape or sand it away. For blobs of glue, use a sharp chisel and gently chip or pare off the glue with the flat back of the chisel against the wood. Hold the blade as flat as possible against the wood to keep the cutting edge from digging in. Sanding off glue takes longer, but it works better for removing smears. Use the next coarser grit than you used for the final sanding to cut through and sand off the glue, then smooth the area out with finer-grit sandpaper. Check your progress by wiping with mineral spirits to ensure you've removed all the glue and sanding scratches. For the final touch-up sanding, be sure to sand with the grain.

Another option for removing dried glue is to re-dissolve it, scrub the softened glue with a synthetic scrubbing pad, and wipe off the residue. Use acetone, toluene, or xylene solvents to soften yellow wood glue. You'll find these chemicals sold in the paint section of your home center or hardware store. Warm water also works, but the stronger solvents offer the added advantage of not raising the wood grain. Acetone also removes hot-melt glue and contact cement. There are no effective solvents for removing polyurethane glue or epoxy. Your only option is to scrape and sand them off.

Filling dents, holes, and other imperfections: You can easily dent bare wood just by dropping it or applying too much clamping pressure. If all the wood in a damaged area is intact but simply compressed, steam out the dent. To do this, wet the damaged area with a few drops of water, cover with a small piece of clean cloth, and heat the cloth with a hot soldering iron or the tip of a clothes iron. As the water on the

If you'd rather not scrape or sand dried glue off, you can also dissolve the excess with a solvent. Use the solvent sparingly, wiping with a synthetic scrub pad. Too much solvent can weaken the glue joint.

Minor dents are easy to remove from bare wood by steaming. Heat a water-dampened cloth in the repair area with the tip of a soldering or clothes iron, and the steam will swell out the blemish.

wood boils, it will swell the wood fibers and virtually eliminate the dent. Be sure to sand the area after it dries to smooth the raised grain.

For repairing holes, use slivers of scrap wood that match the project wood, coat them with a dab of glue, and tap them into the hole. Try to match the grain direction as best you can with these wood plugs. For filling end-grain holes, use end-grain scrap. Face-grain holes should be filled with face-grain scrap. The advantage to using real wood is that the damaged area will take finish just like the surrounding wood and blend in well.

If you fill nailheads after applying stain, choose a tinted wood putty or filler with a color that closely matches the stain color.

A variety of wood doughs, putties, and fillers are also available for filling holes, cracks, and other small imperfections. Basically, these products are mixtures of finely ground wood powder and sawdust blended with glue or lacquer to hold the material together. Most come pre-mixed and ready to use in various wood-tone colors. Although they seem like a convenient solution for making repairs, they don't absorb wood stain well. The patch will be visible, just like a glue smudge, if you apply the filler before staining. If you're planning to stain the project, do this first, then fill the holes with wood putty tinted to blend with the wood stain. Work carefully to keep the repair area as small as possible. The less putty there is to blend with the finish, the easier it will be to conceal.

If the putty has a strong solvent smell when wet, it has a lacquer base. Clean up excess lacquer putty with acetone or lacquer thinner. For products with latex bases, use water to clean up wet putty, and acetone, toluene, or xylene to remove dried putty. Work carefully when cleaning up the excess to keep from removing the wood stain around the repair.

If you have small nail holes to fill, don't worry about concealing these prior to applying finish. After the topcoat dries fully, fill the holes with colored wax. Wax crayons in various wood finish colors are sold in the finishing section of your home center. You can also experiment with ordinary color crayons in the various brown tones. Press a small chip of wax into the hole with a fingernail or paint scraper blade and smooth it with your fingertip. Your body heat will soften the wax and blend it in. Scrape away the excess carefully.

Coloring wood with stains

The topcoat layer of a finish doesn't add much color to the wood. Its primary purpose is to form a protective barrier. To change the color, you'll need to apply stain before the topcoat. Most of the wood you see in furniture has been color-altered with a stain. Stain gives you creative control over how your completed project looks in a three ways: First, it allows you to choose the basic color of the wood from a wide range of color tones. If you'd prefer your mahogany project to look more red or brown than the natural wood, a stain provides the means for making the color shift. Second, it enhances the natural grain pattern in the wood. This is highly desirable in some woods, such as curly maple or quartersawn oak, that have interesting wavy or flake patterns in the grain. It's not always advantageous in other woods, such as pine or soft maple, because the grain density of these woods varies significantly in the same board. Certain types of stains can make the wood look splotchy and uneven. A third reason for staining is that it blends wood with contrasting heartwood and sapwood so the light and dark areas are less pronounced.

The components that give a stain its color are pigments, dyes, or a combination of the two. Pigments are finely-ground particles of colored earth or synthetic chemicals suspended in a liquid. Dyes contain much smaller molecules of color.

Pigments color wood by filling the open pores on the surface. The more pigment that gets trapped in the pores, the darker the grain appears. Once the pores are filled with pigment, the wood can't be made darker with more pigment. Usually one application of pigment stain fills the pores. Pigment-based stains are more effective for coloring open-grained woods, such as mahogany or oak, than for denser, closed-grained woods, such as hard maple. If the pores are too small to trap the pigment, the wood color won't change much.

RAISING THE GRAIN

No matter how smoothly you sand wood surfaces before finishing, water-based dye, stain, or varnish will still raise the wood grain. Here's why: Water-based finishing products soak into the surface fibers of raw wood and cause them to swell up. Once the wood swells, it feels rough and the smoothing effect of sanding is lost. The solution is to raise the grain before applying finish, sand the rough grain off, and then proceed with finishing. To do this, wet your project with distilled water and a damp rag, and let the wood dry for a few hours. Sand lightly with the same grit of paper you used for your final sanding. The paper need not be from a fresh sheet. Used sandpaper abrades less and leaves smaller scratches. Sand just until the wood feels smooth. This step knocks off the raised wood fibers at the surface so the grain can't raise again.

The liquid component of pigment-based stains keeps the pigment suspended and helps the particles of color flow onto the wood easily. There's also a binding agent in the liquid that acts like glue to hold the particles in the pores. Binders are made of water-based acrylic, oil, varnish, or lacquer, depending on the stain chemistry.

Dye stains work differently than pigment-based stains. Since dyes are molecules of color rather than larger particulates, they absorb into the wood's cells. Dyes saturate both open-grained and tight-grained woods relatively evenly. They also color both face and end grain consistently, unlike pigment stains that make end grain much darker. The higher the concentration of dye, the darker the wood color becomes. Dyes can make wood darker than pigments because the coloring action isn't limited by the depth of the surface pores.

Dye stains are commonly sold in powdered form rather than a liquid. You won't find dye powders sold in a hardware store or home center, but they're widely available from woodworking supply catalogs. Dye powders are formulated into both wood tone shades and primary colors. Depending on the chemistry of the powder, dyes need to be mixed with either water or denatured alcohol to create the liquid for staining. The solvent dissolves the dye and helps it flow over the wood. The particular solvent you need to use will be labeled clearly on the container of dye powder. As long as dye powders have the same solvents, you can mix them in any combination you like to make your own custom colors.

Some dye stains are sold premixed as "NGR," or non-grain-raising stains. The main advantage to an NGR stain is that unlike water-soluble dye stains, which raise the grain, NGR stains do not.

Most of the ordinary premixed stains you'll find on the shelves of the hardware store or home center are pigment-based. Some manufacturers mix both pigments and dye into one solution to produce more even coloring characteristics. You can't easily tell on the label whether a premixed stain is only pigment or a mixture of both pigment and dye. Use the stain as though it is primarily pigment-based.

When to use pigments vs. dyes: Both pigment and dye stains are easy to apply. If you are choosing between the two, think in terms of the results you want. One issue to consider is the grain pattern of the wood you are finishing. Oak, for example, has distinctively porous and non-porous face grain. The difference in density between the open-pored and closed-pored regions is what gives stained oak its prominent, face-grain pattern. Using pigment stain on oak dramatizes the difference between the open pores and closed pores. The pigment lodges in the open pores, producing dark areas, but it shades the closed-grain areas much less. A dye stain, on the other hand, saturates both the open- and closed-pored areas more evenly, with less light and dark variation.

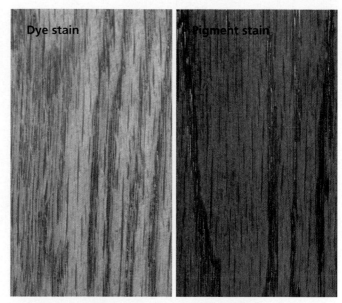

Pigment stain (right) becomes trapped in the open pored areas of oak and darkens them more than dye stain (left). Dye produces more even coloring.

On certain woods, such as pine, birch, and soft maple, the grain pattern isn't as regular and attractive as oak. There can be inconsistent, open-pored areas that aren't easy to see until the stain is applied. Pigment stains make these irregular areas obvious as darker, uneven splotches. For these woods, dye stains blend the surface grains more evenly and minimize splotching. On woods with dramatic figure, such as fiddleback maple, curly cherry, and quartersawn oak and

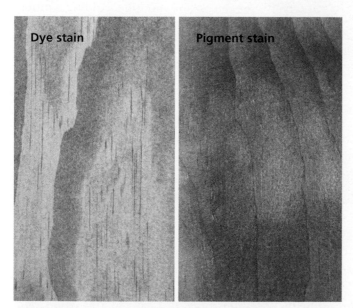

Notice how the pigment stain (right) penetrates unevenly on this pine sample, producing splotches. The left sample was colored with dye.

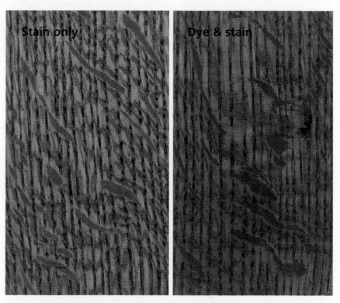

Dye stain applied as a base coat beneath a pigment stain will reveal the contrast of highly figured woods better than pigment stain alone.

Gel stains

If you are staining large vertical surfaces and are concerned about drips, or if you are working with pine or soft maple with inconsistent grain pattern, try a gel stain instead of a liquid. Gel stains are also a great way to match end grain with face grain. Gel stains consist of pigments or dyes suspended in a thick binder of varnish or water-based acrylic. The material typically has the consistency of petroleum jelly and will not flow like a liquid. The coloring agent, whether pigment or dye, doesn't penetrate as deeply into the open pores or cells, and it provides more even coverage on all types of wood. The thinner surface penetration helps minimize blotching and darker end-grain color. However, gel stain can be difficult to control when wiping into corners or crevices. The excess varnish will leave streaks or fill crevices unless it is thoroughly wiped clean. Also, your range of color options is more limited with gel stain than when using conventional, liquid-based pigment or dye stains.

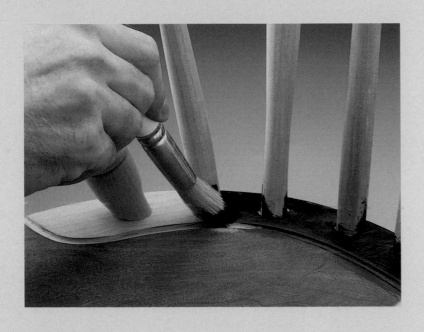

sycamore, dye stain highlights the unique figure. Pigment stains, which don't saturate into the wood fibers, often obscure this depth and contrast. So, dye stains generally are more effective on highly-figured woods.

Dye stain offers more flexibility than pigment stain when it comes to changing the intensity and color once you've stained the project. To lighten a too-dark dye stain, remove the excess color by wiping down the wood surfaces with the same solvent you used to mix the dye powder. The solvent reactivates the dye, and a cloth or paper towel draws it out of the wood cells.

If dye tone or color isn't what you want, you can modify the color by wiping down the project with a different color dye stain or reapplying the same dye and not removing the excess. More dye intensifies the color and tone. Adding a different color dye will blend with the base dye to form a new color.

You can also wipe a coat of pigment stain over the dried dye stain to dramatize the open-grain areas. This is a great technique for finishing figured wood. Use a pigment stain with a different solvent than that of the dye stain to keep the dye from lifting out of the wood. An oil-based pigment stain is a good choice for wiping over water-based dye stain.

One disadvantage to dye stains is that alcohol-based dye stains can fade if wood surfaces are subjected to direct sunlight. Water-based dye stains are more light-fast, but even these fade to a lesser degree over time.

Pigment stains are more difficult to lighten once they are in the wood. The binder acts as a sealing coat over the pigment and holds the pigment in the pores. If you wipe the wood down with the clean-up solvent for the stain while

Aniline dye stains are usually sold in powdered form. To prepare them for use, mix the powder with either distilled water or alcohol, depending on the dye chemistry.

the stain is still wet, it's possible to remove some of the pigment and lighten the color. Once it dries, you'll have to sand the color out.

If you'd like to darken the wood with pigment stain after applying the first coat of stain, apply a second coat and leave the excess on the wood rather than wiping it off. The binder bonds the pigment to the open-pored areas and produces a darker look overall. However, extra pigment will obscure the grain pattern to some degree.

The best way to see what you'll get when using pigment stain versus dye stain is to try both options on a large sample of the same wood you're using for the project. This offers you a chance to try your hand with both stain types and experiment before you commit the stain to the project.

Applying stains

To prepare a pigment stain for application, just stir the can thoroughly. This suspends the pigments and mixes the binder and solvent together. To mix a dye stain, measure and add the dry powder to the appropriate solvent slowly while stirring. For water-based dye, use warm distilled water and stir the mixture until all the powder is blended into solution. Cool water works too, but the powder takes longer to dissolve and can leave clumps.

Pour the stain into a clean, non-metal container. (The stain can react with metal and discolor.) For dye stains, strain the material through a disposable paper paint strainer first to remove any undissolved powder. Prepare enough dye stain to complete your entire project. If you have to mix more midway through, you may introduce color shifts. During the application process, sawdust and other debris will inevitably get mixed with your stain. It's best to dispose of the excess rather than pour it back into the stain can when you are through. Seal the extra stain in a lidded container to keep the solvent from evaporating. Otherwise the binder will thicken and the color intensify as the solvent flashes off. If you'd rather dispose of the extra stain instead of saving it, take oil stains to a hazardous waste drop-off. Water- or alcohol-based dye stains can be safely flushed down the drain with plenty of water.

You can apply stain with a brush, clean rag, or even disposable shop towels. Brushing on stain floods the surface more quickly than wiping, which can help if the stain has a tendency to dry quickly. Wiping on stain is a good way to avoid drips, especially if your project has vertical surfaces.

With the wood surface clean, dry, and smooth, brush or wipe on the stain. Try to cover a complete surface of your project with stain before removing the excess, but don't stain more than one surface at a time to prevent premature drying. Flow the stain on in a moderately heavy coat so the wood surface is thoroughly wet. It doesn't matter if you apply the stain with or across the grain. A heavy flow of pigment stain or dye will fill the pores and color the wood regardless of grain direction. Once the stain is on the wood, wipe off the excess with a clean rag, exposing clean surfaces of the rag as you wipe the surface dry. Work your way across the surface steadily and quickly, wiping each stroke nearly dry before moving onto a new wet area. The goal is to achieve an even-colored film of stain without leaving wiping marks behind. If one dry area looks lighter than another dry area, try wiping your stained rag over the lighter area to apply a bit more stain. If some areas dry prematurely before you have a chance to wipe off

Apply stain with a brush or rag to flood the surface, then wipe off the excess with a clean rag.

Once you've applied stain, it might reveal surface scratches not removed with sanding. Sand these areas again to remove the scratches, then restain.

Choosing a brush for finishing

Brushes are made with either animal-hair or synthetic bristles. You can also find foam-pad brushes. Synthetic bristle brushes perform well with all oil- or water-based stains and topcoats. Avoid using natural-bristle brushes with water-based stains and finishes because the bristles swell and tangle. Foam-pad brushes are inexpensive and save you the hassle of cleaning after use, but they tend to harden or dissolve when used with solvent finishes. Use foam pads with water-based finishes instead.

Brushes between 1½ and 3 inches wide are the most practical sizes for finishing. Choose brushes with bristles about 2 to 3 inches long and with an overall bristle pattern that tapers to a point. Brushes with square edges tend to flow finish unevenly and leave streaks. Look closely at the bristle tips as well. Those that taper to points or splay into fine flagged tips carry more finish than square-tipped bristles.

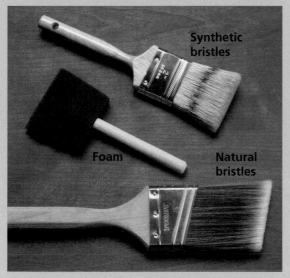

Synthetic bristles work with all finishes, natural bristles work well for oil-based finishes, and foam brushes work well for water-based finishes.

Tapered brushes apply stains more evenly than square brushes.

the excess, try wetting the unwiped areas with the appropriate clean-up thinner (for pigment stains) or the solvent (for dye stains) and then wiping these areas to remove surplus stain.

You'll notice that staining the end grain of wood with pigment stains typically results in a darker color. End grain exposes more wood pores than face or edge grain, which traps more pigment. To help blend the end and face grain color, you may need to apply another coat of stain to the face grain and leave on the excess. This will produce a more even color from face to end grain, but it won't match the two exactly.

Once the excess stain is wiped off and you are pleased with the color, allow the surfaces to dry thoroughly before proceeding with a topcoat of clear finish. After staining, if you notice milling marks or scratches you missed during sanding, remove them now by sanding. Start with a grit one step coarser than your final sanding grit, then switch to the final grit to remove the new sanding scratches. Reapply stain to these areas and blend the color in with the surrounding stain color to hide the repair. It's easier to fix these imperfections now than after the final finish is applied.

Applying a topcoat

There are many finish options for the final topcoat. Among them are wax, oil, wipe-on mixtures of oil and varnish or thinned varnish, unthinned varnish, shellac, and lacquer. Wax alone or a concentrated oil such tung oil or boiled linseed oil are too soft to provide adequate protection from dirt, water penetration, and other incidental surface abrasions. On the other end of the spectrum, lacquer provides a highly durable and protective topcoat, but it's best applied with special spray equipment, and the vapors are both flammable and harmful to breathe. For our purposes here, we'll concentrate on applying the easier, reasonably durable finishes that fall between these extremes: wiping finishes, shellac, and varnish.

WIPE-ON FINISHES

Many, many blends of wiping finishes are marketed to consumers as easy to apply, rapid-drying topcoats. The biggest advantage to using a wipe-on finish is that you can apply these products without ever lifting a brush. All it takes to apply the product is a clean, lint-free rag and some elbow grease. Wipe-on finishes are made from a variety of different ingredients. Some are blends of tung, linseed, or other oils combined with varnish and mineral spirits. Others are basically varnish thinned with mineral spirits so they flow more easily but provide better protection than oil/varnish blends. The product labels rarely identify exactly what concoctions are inside the bottle or can, but you'll know you

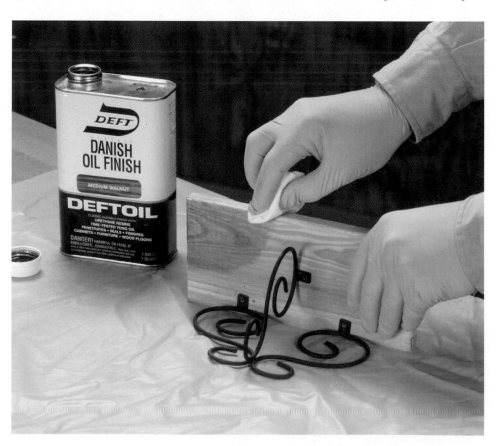

Wipe-on finishes are quick and easy to apply with a clean rag. Allow surfaces to dry between coats of finish.

Untinted wipe-on finishes leave wood looking wet but not shiny. Their thin consistency soaks into wood pores rather than building to a thick film.

Test a wipe-on finish for varnish. If a dried drop of finish dents easily, it is mostly oil. The harder it dries, the more varnish it contains.

are dealing with a wipe-on finish if the product name combines tung oil with varnish, or if the product calls itself a "finish." Products called "Danish," "Scandinavian," or "Nordic" oil finishes are all wipe-on finishes, too.

Wipe-on finishes are not as durable as varnish or shellac that form a protective film on the wood's surface. The finish coat is extremely thin and leaves the wood pores largely exposed. However, for projects that don't require a high level of resistance to moisture or abrasion, wipe-on finishes provide a quick, no-fuss topcoat. Most produce a flat or satin sheen. If you don't want your project to look plasticized or coated with finish, wipe-on finishes may be good options. The downside to wipe-on finishes is that some cure to only a soft coating. The more coats you apply and the thicker the topcoat gets, the softer it will feel. Wipe-on finishes that have a higher percentage of varnish than oil will cure harder, but the varnish is still so thin that it takes several coats to build up the same level of protection as one coat of brushed-on, un-thinned varnish.

Applying a wipe-on finish: Pour a small amount of finish onto a clean, lint-free rag and wipe on the finish until the surface is wet. Allow the finish a few minutes to flow into the pores, then wipe off the excess and allow the surfaces to dry. Leaving excess finish on the wood may seem like an easy way to expedite the finishing process, but it really just prolongs the curing time. You'll get more coats of finish on the wood in less time by wiping off the residue. In humid weather, apply the finish in a well-ventilated but dry area. It can help to run a dehumidifier to lower humidity levels so the finish cures more rapidly. The drier and warmer the air, the faster the finish will cure.

Once the first layer of finish cures, you can apply additional coats of finish to help protect the wood. This is especially effective for thinned varnishes that cure hard even when built up in multiple layers. One way to help identify whether you are using an oil/varnish blended finish or a thinned varnish finish is to put a drop of finish on a piece of scrap, spread it slightly, and allow it

Shellac builds to a smooth film and fills wood pores. Amber shellac casts an orange tone, while blonde shellac cures clear.

to cure. If the drop hardens to the point that you can't dent it with a fingernail, you're using a varnish thinned with mineral spirits. If the finish remains slightly soft, even after curing, it's an oil/varnish blend.

SHELLAC

Another finish that's easy to apply and more durable than wipe-on finishes is shellac. Shellac is a natural resin harvested from purified bug secretions that are dried into a thin sheets and broken into flakes. Used for centuries as a fine furniture finish, shellac is non-toxic in dry form, and it creates a reasonably durable surface film for projects that do not come in contact with water or alcohol. Shellac is usually brushed or sprayed onto wood. The finish can be built up into as many layers as you like for improved surface protection or if you prefer a highly smooth surface on your project. One big advantage to using shellac over some other finishes is that you don't have to sand between one coat and the next. Each new coat of finish partially dissolves the coat beneath and fuses to it for a strong bond.

Another attribute of shellac is that it forms an effective barrier against water vapor exchange in the wood. Shellac helps to reduce the amount of expansion and contraction that always occurs in wood with changes in humidity. You'll appreciate this benefit on projects with doors and drawers. In summer months, less wood expansion means doors and drawers won't swell enough to stick and bind in their openings.

Shellac does have a few downsides. It can be damaged by water, which leaves whitish stains on the wood. These are the familiar drinking glass rings you've probably seen on tabletops finished with shellac. Shellac dissolves in the presence of concentrated alcohol lye, and ammonia. It also softens when exposed to high heat. Use another finish for kitchen or bathroom projects.

Shellac has a natural orange color, but it's also available in formulations with the orange color bleached out. Orange shellac gives wood a warm, amber color when it dries, while bleached varieties cure nearly clear. Most shellac has a percentage of naturally occurring wax in the mixture, which imparts a slightly cloudy tone to the finish. Some finishing techniques use shellac as a sealing coat under other finishes, like varnish. In these cases, the natural wax can cause adhesion problems with the varnish, so shellac is also sold in "dewaxed" form.

Shellac is sold as premixed liquid, in aerosol form, or as dry flakes, as shown below.

Garnet

Blond

You'll find shellac sold in dry flakes or as a premixed liquid in cans and aerosols. Flake shellac must be mixed with denatured alcohol to dissolve the flakes and prepare it for use. The advantage to starting with flakes over pre-mixed varieties is that the flakes have a much longer shelf life. Dry flake shellac will last for several years or more, but a can of pre-mixed liquid shellac is only good for about one year, and even less after it's opened. As liquid or aerosol shellac ages, it takes longer to cure and eventually won't cure at all. If you buy liquid shellac rather than flakes, you can check its freshness with a fingernail test just like you would with a drop of wipe-on finish (see page 135).

Blend shellac flakes in a non-metal container with denatured alcohol to prepare it for use. The ratio of flakes to solvent establishes the mixture's "cut".

Preparing shellac for use: Mixing dry flake shellac with alcohol is called "cutting" the shellac. "Cut" refers to the number of pounds of shellac that are dissolved into one gallon of denatured alcohol. This quantity of alcohol is only a universal starting point. Actually, you can mix any quantity of shellac you need, no matter how small, using smaller increments of shellac and alcohol. Premixed liquid shellac is commonly sold in 3- to 5-pound cuts. The higher the number, the greater the percentage of shellac in alcohol and the thicker the mixture is. For general finishing, a 2-pound cut is ideal. It spreads easily with a brush and produces an even surface film with each coat. You can obtain this blend by diluting premixed shellac with denatured alcohol or by mixing flake shellac in the correct proportions with alcohol. Information is printed on the shellac can for diluting premixed shellac for a variety of cuts. If the can doesn't specify how to make thinner cuts, mix ½ part alcohol to one part premixed shellac for making a 2-pound cut.

When you're starting with flake shellac, here's how to prepare a reasonable quantity of 2-pound cut for finishing smaller projects: Combine one pint of denatured alcohol with ¼ pound (4 ounces) of shellac flakes. Mix the two together in a glass or plastic container. Metal containers will react with the shellac and discolor it. Stir the solution thoroughly until all the flakes are dissolved in the alcohol and then stir periodically during use to keep the shellac from clumping.

Strain freshly blended shellac through a paper filter to remove bits of undissolved shellac before use.

Once the shellac and alcohol are thoroughly blended together, strain the liquid through a disposable paint strainer into a clean container to remove bits of undissolved shellac. Keep the container covered with a tight lid when not in use to prevent the alcohol from absorbing water from the air. Label the container with the date you prepared it in case you need to store an unused portion for use later.

Brush on shellac in long, overlapping strokes keeping the edges between the strokes wet. Allow each coat to dry thoroughly before reapplying.

Applying a shellac finish: The alcohol solvent in shellac evaporates quickly, which is good for efficiency's sake but somewhat challenging if you have a large surface to cover. The trick to brushing shellac is to keep the surface wet. The area you are brushing should contact the area you've just brushed along a wet edge. This way, the brush won't drag over partially dried shellac and leave ridges. Move the brush in long, overlapping strokes in the direction of the wood grain. Keep the brush moving over the wood, and reload the brush as soon as the shellac stops flowing out smoothly. You can use either a synthetic or natural bristle brush and get good results. If the 2-pound cut seems too thick to brush easily over the bare wood, thin it to a 1-pound cut instead. A thinner cut may also be helpful if you notice small bubbles appearing in the finish that don't pop as the shellac cures. However, be aware that a thinner cut will dry faster than a thicker cut—it contains more alcohol.

After you've brushed on the first coat, allow at least two hours of drying time before applying the second coat. Then brush the second coat right over the first with no further prep work. Alcohol in the second coat will dissolve the first coat slightly, and the two layers of finish will bond together well. Apply as many additional coats of shellac as you like to "build up" the surface smoothness.

VARNISH

Of all the topcoat options available to consumers, varnish is the usual choice, and it's a good one. It forms a tough, protective film on the wood surface, and some varieties are highly resistant to wear, heat, acids, and solvents. Varnish is easy to apply with a brush, but it cures much more slowly than shellac. Once cured, varnish behaves like a coating of plastic over the wood, sealing the pores and helping to reduce wood movement. Another advantage to varnish is that you can buy it formulated to cure to flat, satin, or gloss sheens. This way, you can use varnish to simulate a "close-to-the-wood" finish that doesn't shine, a finish with just a bit of sheen to it, or a highly wet-looking finish. You can reduce the sheen of gloss varnish by rubbing the cured finish with #0000 steel wool and mineral spirits to whatever level of sheen you prefer.

The term varnish encompasses a variety of products, but they can be broken into three broad categories: alkyd varnish, polyurethane varnish, and water-based acrylic or

Varnish dries to various surface sheens including satin, semi-gloss, and gloss. However, a gloss varnish can be dulled to lesser sheens by rubbing it with steel wool or fine abrasives.

water-based polyurethane. The first two varnish types are made by combining various oils with blends of synthetic resins and metallic driers to help accelerate the curing process. Water-based varnishes are mixtures of acrylic or polyurethane and water. Oil-based varnishes are more resistant to water, solvents, and heat than water-based products, but the wet varnish creates unpleasant fumes as it cures. Oil-based varnishes take on a yellowish tint as they age, and the polyurethane can leave an amber tint. Polyurethane also degrades in the presence of ultraviolet sunlight. Over time, poly varnish will eventually peel off the wood if its exposed to direct sunlight. Some polyurethane formulations have UV additives to help counteract this tendency.

The popularity of varnish with consumers is evident in the wide range of products available. You'll find stain/varnish mixes, water- or oil-based formulations, aerosols, gels, and wipe-on varnish.

Among the oil-based varnishes, you'll find some labeled as "spar" or "marine" varnishes intended for outdoor applications. These blends are made with oils that prevent the varnish from curing to a hard film like other varnishes made for interior projects. The softer cure of a spar varnish makes it more flexible. This characteristic is important for wood exposed to the elements because the wood expands and contracts more than it would if stored indoors. Soft varnish is better able to move with the wood. For a tougher finish, go with an interior varnish.

Oil-based varnishes also come in gel forms with working characteristics similar to gel-based stains. The varnish wipes on with a cloth instead of brushing. It's handy for use on vertical surfaces where liquid varnishes could drip, run, or sag. The best areas for applying gel varnish are flat, open surfaces without small details or inside corners. The gel can be difficult to apply evenly in these areas and can leave globs.

Water-based varnish has different characteristics than its oil-based cousins. It is more susceptible to damage from solvents, water, and heat. It dries to a highly scratch resistant coating, much harder than oil-based polyurethane and about equal to alkyd varnish. You'll need to raise the grain and sand the wood smooth before applying water-based varnish (see page 127). Otherwise, the varnish will raise the grain as it soaks into the surface. Water-based polyurethane dries clear and takes no yellowish cast over time, although some finishers feel that it leaves wood looking dull and without depth. Probably the biggest advantage to using water-based varnish is its low solvent content. It emits significantly fewer bad-smelling fumes, and the curing varnish isn't a fire hazard as the solvents evaporate. Clean-up is also easier. Wash brushes in warm, soapy water before the varnish cures.

The lower solvent content of water-based varnish makes it easier on your nose, but it's more likely to leave undissolved bits in the can. Strain it through a paper filter before using.

Applying a varnish finish: Both oil- and water-based varnishes can be applied with a synthetic bristle brush. Use natural-bristle brushes with oil-based varnishes only. Water-based varnish will swell and tangle natural bristles. Because varnish cures slowly, especially oil-based varnish, it's important to work in a clean, dust-free environment. Otherwise, bits of dust in the air will settle on the varnish before it cures and leave tiny rough spots on the surface. It's a good idea to apply varnish away from the workshop in another room to avoid these dust issues. Work in a well-ventilated area. If you are sensitive to concentrated solvent fumes, wear a cartridge-style respirator.

For the first coat of finish, many experts thin oil-based varnish to a 50/50 mixture with mineral spirits. The thinned varnish spreads more easily with a brush over bare wood. If you're using water-based varnish, there's no need to thin the first coat. Its composition is thinner than oil-based varnish right out of the can, and it flows easily. Strain water-based varnish through a paper filter before applying it. The low solvent content makes water-based varnish more likely to have bits of undissolved solids in the liquid.

With either varnish, pour off a small amount of finish from the can into a clean container and load the brush from this container. To brush on the varnish, start a few inches in from the ends of the surface and brush out to the ends. Apply these short brush strokes with the grain. Starting in from the end and working outward helps you avoid leaving extra varnish right on the ends of the surface where it can run or drip. Once both ends of the surface are covered, brush the bare area in between in long, overlapping strokes. When the whole surface is covered with wet finish, drag just the tips of the bristles over the surface in long strokes to level any ridges and dips. This technique is called "tipping off" the finish, and it also helps pop small bubbles in the surface film before they cure hard. Skim the bristles against the edge of the finishing container to remove any excess after each tip-off stroke. Let the first layer of finish cure hard.

When the varnish is dry, sand it lightly with 280-grit paper. For water-based varnish, this sanding knocks off any grain nibs that may have raised up through the first coat of finish. On oil-based varnish, especially polyurethane, sanding between coats is crucial. It abrades the varnish film just enough so the next coat can form a mechanical connection to the coat underneath. Varnish is not like shellac, which partially dissolves the finish layer beneath and forms a chemical connection. Clean off all sanding dust and grit with a vacuum or compressed air.

Apply the next coat of varnish, just as you did for the first coat, keeping a wet edge and brushing with the grain. After this coat dries hard, prepare it for another coat by sanding lightly with 320- or finer-grit sandpaper to scuff the surface film. You can also use a fine-textured synthetic scrub pad for this purpose. Look for pads colored grey or white—the green ones are too coarse. Clean the surfaces before brushing the varnish. For most applications, two to three coats of varnish builds a sufficiently durable finish. However, you can apply as many coats as you like, provided you sand lightly between coats.

Apply varnish by brushing short strokes out to the edges of a workpiece first. This minimizes drips and sags along the edges. Then fill in the center area with long, even strokes, tipping off the finish when it's fully applied.

PAINTED FINISHES

If wood grain and texture aren't important for a project, paint makes a wonderful finish. It provides durable protection against surface abrasions, spills, and degradation from UV sunlight. Now that all paint is lead-free, it's child-safe when dry and you can't beat the vibrant color choices. Exterior paint is the best of all finishes for outdoor wood projects; it will outlast spar varnish if applied correctly. Paint usually won't peel unless it is applied without a primer coat, used over wet wood, or subjected to standing water.

Both oil- and water-based paints are good choices for wood. Oil-based paints take longer to dry, but some experts prefer them because of their smooth-flowing and leveling tendencies. Acrylic latex paint is just as durable as oil-based paint, and it comes in the same sheen options. Latex paint is also easy to clean up with soapy water. Some experts also argue that latex paint provides a more flexible coating over wood than oil paint, so it won't crack or peel as the wood moves.

All varieties of lumber you'll find at the home center can be painted. Closed-grain woods such as birch, maple, and poplar provide the smoothest surface for paint. If you paint cedar, pine, or redwood, use a primer fortified with additives that help seal in natural oils and pitch to keep the these substances from bleeding through the paint and staining it. Many exotic woods, such as teak, cocobolo, and rosewood, are extremely oily and are not good candidates for a painted finish.

Prepare bare wood for paint just as you would for stains and clear topcoats. Sand the surfaces thoroughly up to 150- or 180-grit, remove all dust, and raise the grain if you're using a water-based paint. Apply the recommended primer for the paint with a bristle or foam brush. Primer serves several important purposes: It levels the wood surface, seals the pores, and allows the paint to bond fully with the wood. Never skip the primer, or you'll compromise the finish.

Once the primer dries, topcoat with two or more coats of paint. You only need to apply enough coats of paint to form an even surface color. Protective properties of paint don't improve with more than a few layers. Apply each coat sparingly so it dries quickly and doesn't drip or sag. There's no need to sand between coats.

Painted finishes always begin with a base layer of primer. Use a primer that's compatible with the oil- or latex-based paint you will use as a topcoat.

When the primer dries, overcoat with paint. One or two coats should be enough to produce an even surface color.

INDEX